"Most people spend their entire lives counting down the days until their next one-week vacation, but fortunately, life doesn't have to be like that! Take it from Alexa West. She is one of the early digital nomad pioneers who discovered how to transform her travels from a short-lived vacation into an everyday lifestyle. She is a true leader in the space and an amazing example for all travelers who dream of booking that one-way ticket and living their daily life from the road."

— **Christian LeBlanc**, creator of Lost LeBlanc
and Lost Creator Academy

"If I could go back in time and give my younger self this book, maybe she would have felt less alone in her choices to start traveling full-time."

— **Beth Johnstone**, professional nomad
and creator at She Is the Lost Girl

"*The One-Way Ticket Plan* will have you laughing, crying, and ditching your 9-to-5 for a lifestyle you love."

— **Valerie Joy Wilson**, travel expert
and founder of Trusted Travel Girl

"Solo travel is the most transformative experience women can give themselves. This is the bible on how to do it right."

— **Christina Galbato**, entrepreneur
and online marketing expert

"Proof that you can make money from anywhere in the world, even in your bathing suit on a beach."

— **Karlie Cummins**, founder of Bali Buddies

"Alexa West wants you 'to see that the concept of "the real world" is fake and the whole world is real.' *That's* why women should travel before and/or instead of rushing into jobs and marriage and kids — because travel teaches you that you are brave enough to do whatever it takes to find your own most inspiring version of your life, instead of falling into the first life that presents itself out of fear."

— **Kristin Newman**, author of
What I Was Doing While You Were Breeding

"The bible for solo female travelers."

"This book is a must-have for every woman who has ever thought, *I want to pack everything up and travel the world to be wild and free. The One-Way Ticket Plan* is the ultimate guide for making your travel dreams a reality. It's fun, relatable, and most importantly, filled with easy and actionable tips. All you have to do is pick it up, and you'll be ready to start exploring the world. As Alexa West says, 'the best adventures start with the simple decision to go,' so go read this book and be on your way!"

— **Arden Joy**, founder of Girls Who Travel
and author of *Keep This Off the Record* (forthcoming)

"*The One-Way Ticket Plan* is a wonderful resource to help new and experienced travelers start planning and navigating every step of their journey."

— **Jen Moyse**, vice president of product
and head of UX at TripIt

"I wish I'd had this book when I was eighteen and venturing out into the world on my own — maybe it wouldn't have taken me ten years to find my purpose! As someone who felt pressure to go to college, get married, and settle down before my late twenties (and trust me, I did that), I only found myself miserable and wanting more out of life. Thankfully, ten years later, I got a second chance. This book, however, would have saved me those years of doubt and fear that kept me from pursuing my dreams from the start."

— **Alicia Taylor**, founder of Cherry Bombs

"This book shows women so much more than just how to get the courage to travel solo; it's a road map to self-discovery and personal growth. It will empower women to step out of their comfort zones and embrace their passions, not just while traveling."

— **Katy Nastro**, travel expert and spokesperson at Going.com

THE
ONE-WAY
TICKET PLAN

ALSO BY ALEXA WEST

The Solo Girl's Travel Guide: Baja Sur

The Solo Girl's Travel Guide: Bali

The Solo Girl's Travel Guide: Cambodia

The Solo Girl's Travel Guide: Japan

The Solo Girl's Travel Guide: Mexico City

The Solo Girl's Travel Guide:
Puerto Vallarta and the Riviera Nayarit

The Solo Girl's Travel Guide: Seattle

The Solo Girl's Travel Guide: Singapore

The Solo Girl's Travel Guide: Southeast Asia

The Solo Girl's Travel Guide: South Korea

The Solo Girl's Travel Guide: Spain

The Solo Girl's Travel Guide: Thailand

The Solo Girl's Travel Guide: Thailand Islands and Beaches

The Solo Girl's Travel Guide: Vietnam

And more to come…

THE
ONE-WAY
TICKET PLAN

FIND AND FUND
YOUR PURPOSE WHILE
TRAVELING THE WORLD

ALEXA WEST

New World Library
Novato, California

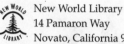 New World Library
14 Pamaron Way
Novato, California 94949

Copyright © 2023 by Alexa West

Text design by Emilia Igartua
Typography by Tona Pearce Myers

Library of Congress Cataloging-in-Publication data is available.

First printing, September 2023
ISBN 978-1-60868-870-8
Ebook ISBN 978-1-60868-871-5
Printed in Canada on 100% postconsumer-waste recycled paper

 New World Library is proud to be a Gold Certified Environmentally Responsible Publisher. Publisher certification awarded by Green Press Initiative.

10   9   8   7   6   5   4   3   2   1

You have brains in your head.
You have feet in your shoes.
You can steer yourself any direction you choose.

— DOCTOR SEUSS

Contents

PART 1: THE ESCAPE PLAN

PART 2: SURVIVING AND THRIVING

PART 3: YOUR EXIT STRATEGY

PART 4: STAYING AND GOING

PART 5: LIFE IS SHORT

PART ONE

THE ESCAPE PLAN

CHAPTER 1

You're a Traveler Now

I knew that I was making a real difference in the world the day a girl messaged me in the middle of the night from Indonesia in a potty panic.

She had been holding it in for three days because the only toilets she could find were squatty potties. You know, the holes in the ground that you squat over and flush with a bucket. She was suffering and needed my advice immediately. I told her she had three options:

1. Hire a driver and give him the mission of driving around Sumatra looking for a Western toilet. Tell him to call everyone he knows to find one.
2. Go in the jungle. Be an animal.
3. Use the damn squatty potty.

I withheld mentioning that if she used the squatty potty, she'd likely have to spray her bum with a hose that we call the "bum gun" or handwash with a bucket of water — both of which accompany most squatty potties in Asia rather than toilet paper. I knew she'd figure this out on her own as using a squatty potty is actually way more intuitive than your fear would like you to believe.

In the end, she squatted and survived. Not only has she conquered one of the biggest travel challenges for Western folk, but she now knows what to do the next time there are no sit-down toilets around.

Honestly, I am not a fan of toilet humor, but you've got to have a little toilet humor to travel the world.

Talking about toilets is not the most glamorous way to start this book, I know, but it's one of the most real travel lessons I can give you — and that's my goal. To make you feel prepared for the intimidating or embarrassing things that otherwise might hold you back from ever leaving home. I want you to recognize that what you have to gain is greater than the obstacles you have to overcome.

So yeah, this is what I do.

Hi, I'm Lexi. I'm the author and founder of The Solo Girl's Travel Guide, the bestselling travel guidebook series for women. It is my actual job to travel around the world making mistakes and learning lessons to pass on to my readers. I'm an expert in how to avoid scams, creeps, and sketchy situations — but I'm also an expert in overcoming your travel fears so that you can access life's most beautiful experiences.

All day every day, I get messages from women around the world in panicky situations like these:

◆ A woman whose purse and phone were stolen by a monkey.

◆ A woman who wanted to leave Bali because it was raining.

◆ A woman who was too afraid to board her plane for Thailand ... while at the gate for her plane to Thailand.

◆ A woman with a rash in a place so intimate she couldn't take a picture to show me.

When these women have questions, I have answers. When they have problems, I have solutions. When they face challenges, I help them find the gift in their lessons. When they have success stories, I am over here waiting to applaud them because I know how it feels to step outside your comfort zone to do something big.

What makes me such a travel expert? Well, at the age of twenty-two, I sat on my bedroom floor, packed my whole life into a big-ass backpack, and flew to the other side of the world on a one-way ticket with just $200 in my pocket. I had zero solo travel experience and no idea what the hell I was doing, but I knew I wanted to do big things. What big things? I wasn't clear on that. The only clarity I had was that I wanted more than just surviving and struggling and hustling until I retired. I wanted to chase life immediately. I wanted to get lost, speak new languages, try new food, swim naked in the ocean, walk barefoot in the forest, fall down, get up, kiss strangers, and create my own version of what a "happy life" looked like. And I did.

For the past thirteen years and counting, I've been living abroad, traveling nonstop. Riding motorbikes through the jungles of Thailand, tending bar barefoot on islands in Cambodia, teaching English in South Korea, healing my childhood trauma in Bali, house-sitting in Costa Rica, and eating *tacos de cabeza* in Mexico — all while discovering who I am and what I want.

This is what I want for you.

I want you to see that the concept of "the real world" is fake and the whole world is real. You don't have to limit your life to the country where you were born. You can build a future, make money, and fall in love (with people, passions, and yourself) from anywhere on the planet.

I am proof that your dream life can be your real life and you ain't gotta be rich to do it. No matter how much money is in your bank account, this whole travel-the-world thing is a lot more accessible than you might think. There are opportunities available to you right now that could whisk you away to a new reality, and you don't even have to sell your organs or join a pyramid scheme to make it happen.

Whatever box you're stuck in, travel is a ladder to help you climb out.

You don't have to wait until you're retired or have $20,000 in the bank to travel the world. Even if you have credit card debt or student loans, I'll show you ways to pay it down while you travel. This isn't a gimmick. I'm not an influencer trying to sell you an unrealistic dream. I'm a real girl who came from nothing, raised by a single mother who struggled to pay the bills, and I used travel to create a life that I'd thought was only reserved for trust fund babies.

No matter if you're in college trying to figure out what's next, if you're getting divorced at thirty-five, or if you're further down the road — the truth remains that you have countless options to flip your life upside down and start over, or just do something different for a while.

Oh, and by the way, I have a not-so-hidden agenda that you'll soon come to notice. In this book, I talk about solo travel often. By the time you've finished reading, I plan to have convinced you to travel alone at least once in your life. But take a deep breath and let me tell you that I also celebrate the idea of traveling with your partner, with your best friend, and with your family. Each experience is completely unique, but solo travel is where the most powerful growth and revelations occur. So don't be afraid when I nudge you toward solo travel. Just stay open to the idea, no matter how scary it might seem right now.

Yes, travel can be challenging, especially solo travel. I have never been kidnapped, but I have been broke, sick, lonely, and lost. But with each lesson, I was given an opportunity to discover just how resilient I am — and you will, too. Embrace these lessons. They will transform you into who you are meant to be.

Still, I wish I could go back in time and give this book to younger me. If younger me had this book in her hands, she would have begun planning her travel path in high school. She would have made money faster, spent money slower, and definitely put less emphasis and urgency on the fairy tale of getting married and settling down.

I do want to clarify one thing, though: If you married your high school sweetheart and had kids in your twenties, this was part of your purpose and that's beautiful. But when you're ready for the next chapter of your life, this book is here waiting for you. Self-discovery doesn't stop at kids or marriage or retirement.

To illustrate this point, let me share a quick story from my dear friend and exquisite writer, Sharon.

The first time I traveled alone I was forty-eight years old and newly divorced. I'd married before I finished school, had kids early, had several careers, and was happy. I was lucky enough to travel with my husband and children and enjoyed making sure they got what they wanted out of our trips. When my husband left, I was determined I wouldn't lose travel along with my marriage, so I booked a trip to Paris. Daunted by the prospect of twenty-one meals in a row alone, I packed a suitcase full of books for company.

My first morning in Paris I woke to pouring rain and lay in bed trying to decide how I'd spend my day. As I struggled to settle on a plan, it dawned on me that during the years I'd spent taking care of everyone else, I'd given my longing away. The only desire I could identify was that whatever else happened that day, I didn't want to have cold, wet feet, and the only shoes I had were the sandals I'd worn on the plane. As the rain fell, I did something I'd never have been able to do on a family trip: I ignored Paris, made a pot of tea, got back in bed, and read until the rain stopped. When it did, I went out and bought myself a pair of warm shoes and socks. Traveling alone helped me learn how to want again.

So what will be revealed for you when you're on the other side of the world, away from everyone and everything you've ever known? What revelation will rise to the surface on a stormy night in the jungle when the power goes out and all you're left to do is sit and stare at the thatched roof above you? What will you daydream about on the plane, and what will you fantasize about in the shower when you're untethered from your usual distractions? What version of you is waiting on the other side of the world?

It's time to go find out.

Please understand that I'm not asking you to change your identity, renounce your citizenship, buy a one-way ticket, and never come back. The goal here isn't to abandon everything and everyone you love. The goal is to go out into the world and be oh so very intentional in getting to know yourself again while discovering new possibilities for your life.

Maybe you'll wander the world until you die, or maybe you'll travel for a month and decide that life in your city is perfectly fulfilling. Maybe you'll come home with a list of places that will have you traveling for the rest of time, or maybe you'll come home happy with one small but important ritual — say, afternoon tea with scones and clotted cream — that will remind you of the woman you discovered far from home. Maybe you'll go to places even I haven't been, or maybe you'll only travel to places where the hotels have sit-down toilets. It doesn't matter how your one-way ticket ends or how your trip goes; it just matters that it begins.

✈ **TRAVEL LESSON #1** ·····································

Every woman should travel solo at least once in her life if only to learn how strong she is on her own.

··

You don't need a boyfriend, a travel partner, or anyone's approval to travel the world. And you don't need a massive bank account or an entire summer off work. If you've doubted yourself for one moment, remember this: Millions of girls travel across the globe all by themselves every damn day, and you can, too. You are just as capable, just as smart, and just as brave as the rest of us. You don't need permission to go — this is your life.

You're not too old, you're not too young. It isn't too early, it isn't too late. If you're reading this book, you're right on time.

This is your sign.

CHAPTER 2

Pick Your Travel Path

Imagine this: Weeks from right now, you could be living in Costa Rica rent-free. Or wandering night markets in South Korea after a day of teaching. Or building your graphic design agency from your laptop in Portugal. Or taking your career as a hairdresser to Bali.

These are just a few examples of the unlimited opportunities available to you right now. Opportunities that have the power to transform your life overnight if you just say yes to one of them.

Sound too good to be true? There's no catch, I promise. I'm not going to suggest you become an Instagram model or sell pictures of your feet online. This is all legit. There are real jobs, lucrative careers, and fun financial avenues all around the world that most people don't know exist, waiting for you right now.

I call these opportunities Travel Paths. Travel Paths are all the ways you can make money, start a career, sustain your travels, discover your purpose, or just get a roof over your head while clearing your mind for a few months under the sun. Some paths have a defined ending, while others are *Alice in Wonderland* rabbit holes with twists and turns you could never predict.

Think of this chapter like speed dating: I'm going to quickly introduce you to these Travel Paths, and when you meet one that makes you feel tingly inside, you can choose to get to know it better, later.

There are no limits to these paths. They are customizable. You can use them now or revisit them ten years from now as most of these paths are not age specific. For example, when I was in the Peace Corps at age twenty-two, I was one of the youngest volunteers in my group, while the oldest volunteer was a grandmother from Texas in her late sixties. So no excuses. Nothing you're about to read is too big or out of reach. You can do and have anything you want, no matter how well your knees still do or do not work.

At the end of this chapter, you'll find a visual flow chart to see exactly how I've been traveling the world for so many years. Then, I'll help you create a vision for how you want to travel the world, too.

Thought Break

Take out a piece of paper and make a list of the following (I'm serious — do it):

o   **Skills:** List your skills. Include all the things that might be considered unique in other countries, including the languages you speak and the cookies you make.
o   **Loves:** List what you enjoy doing. What makes you happiest? Being in water? Working with kids?
o   **Hates:** List what you hate doing. Being in water? Working with kids?
o   **Timeframe:** List how long you want to or are able to travel. A month? A year? Forever and ever?

Keep these things in mind as you read each Travel Path, but don't think too hard. For now, just start reading and daydream. Dream as big as you can. Figure out what feels good.

✈ **TRAVEL LESSON #2** ·······································

If it makes you nervous, it's probably worth it.

···

Nervous is good. Nervous is big. Nervous means that you're about to do something out of your comfort zone that excites you a little. Don't be afraid of nervous.

By the way, Travel Lesson #2 is a lyric from the unofficial official theme song to this book, "Daydream" by Lily Meola. Listen to it as soon and as often as possible.

Travel Paths, summarized in the graphic below, are categorized by motivation. Several of them may match your

✈ **TRAVEL PATHS** ···································

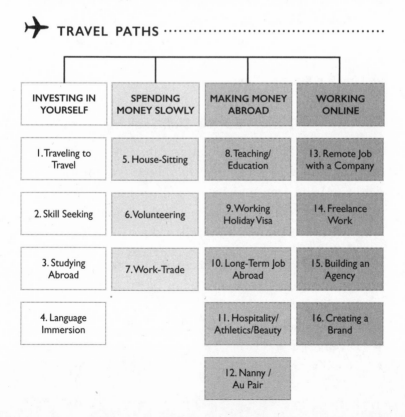

INVESTING IN YOURSELF	SPENDING MONEY SLOWLY	MAKING MONEY ABROAD	WORKING ONLINE
1. Traveling to Travel	5. House-Sitting	8. Teaching/ Education	13. Remote Job with a Company
2. Skill Seeking	6. Volunteering	9. Working Holiday Visa	14. Freelance Work
3. Studying Abroad	7. Work-Trade	10. Long-Term Job Abroad	15. Building an Agency
4. Language Immersion		11. Hospitality/ Athletics/Beauty	16. Creating a Brand
		12. Nanny / Au Pair	

motivations right now, and several may match your motivations in the years to come. You'll never run out of paths to follow, depending on the needs you have and when you have them. As you read, take note of which paths fulfill your immediate needs.

Are you ready? Let's go.

MOTIVATION: INVESTING IN YOURSELF

Travel Path #1: Traveling to Travel

Perhaps you're totally content with the dynamics of your life at home but want to travel longer than a week or travel beyond the walls of an all-inclusive resort. You do not have to be looking for a new job or to permanently move cities for this Travel Paths chapter to be beneficial to you. I'm about to reveal some unconventional ways to travel, which will lead you toward places and purposes you never knew you were looking for. Keep reading.

Travel Path #2: Skill Seeking

Take your passion and turn it into a career by getting accredited or certified in something that allows you to travel the world and find a job anywhere.

No matter where I am in the world, I run into travelers studying to become one of the following:

- ESL (English as a second language) teacher
- Yoga teacher
- Makeup artist
- Massage therapist
- Divemaster
- Free-diver

- ◆ Chef
- ◆ Hospitality professional

Why are these professions so popular? Because they allow you to live and make money anywhere in the world and (aside from ESL teaching) are not solely reserved for English speakers. Even more appealing, perhaps, is that these accreditation programs double as an adventure.

For example, want to be a yoga teacher? Go to India, enroll in a 200-hour yoga teacher training program, stay for a month, learn, explore, make new friends, and leave with the tools to begin a career.

The only caution I'd give you is to be aware of how competitive landing a job in that field might be. Don't think that just because you studied to become a divemaster in Thailand you'll immediately land a divemaster job in Thailand. These gigs can be competitive. Before you spend $2,000 on an accreditation, make a plan. Study up on how you can turn this training into a real job. Speak to the training schools to see if they offer support in finding jobs after you complete the program.

Want to be an English teacher abroad? Many ESL or TEFL (teaching English as a foreign language) programs train you in Japan or Malaysia or somewhere equally exhilarating, and once you complete the training, they match you with a teaching job in the region. Pretty cool, right?

Moral of the story: Before you invest your time, money, hopes, and dreams into a skill-set program, play around with a possible three-year plan. Have a trajectory or at least find some examples of people who have done what you want to do. Or make your own path. As my best friend Emilia always says, "When they go left, we go right." Host your own yoga retreats, start your own massage business, or become a private chef on a goddamn yacht. Creativity will take you places.

Travel Path #3: Studying Abroad

I used to think studying abroad was for rich kids, but with scholarships and grants, you can fund your studies and fund your travels in an economical way. My least favorite American ex-boyfriend got his master's degree in Oslo, Norway — for free. Whatever you can afford, here's the way I see it: If you're going to pay money to go to school, why not pay a school that doubles as a cultural experience abroad? Or better yet, hunt down programs that will completely fund your studies, and don't pay anything at all.

▶ *How to Find Study Abroad Programs*

1. **If you're already studying, ask your department or school if they have exchange programs.** Many academic departments — from business to art history to foreign languages — have exchange partners abroad.
2. **Directly enroll in a university program abroad.** Many universities worldwide accept international students and even offer grants or scholarships.
3. **Use a program-finder website.** GoOverseas.com and other sites like it list degree programs and exchanges, plus guide you on how to apply.
4. **Intern abroad.** Spend your summer working for a marketing consulting firm in Australia or an investment group in Switzerland. Travel, fulfill school credit requirements, and get ahead of the pack with a killer résumé. Check out GoOverseas.com/internships -abroad for practically every internship opportunity under the sun.

For scholarships, also check out GoOverseas.com. They'll often have a list of the most up-to-date scholarship programs abroad. Really, just start with that website in general. They make this whole study-abroad process super simple.

Fun program recommendation: Semester at Sea. This is a program where you live on a cruise ship with students from universities worldwide and visit multiple countries while completing your semester of studies. Not a college student? Semester at Sea also offers programs for gap year students (the year in between high school and college), recent college grads, and "lifelong learners" of any age. PS. I'm usually not a fan of big cruise ships, but Semester at Sea is heavily committed to sustainability on land and sea and setting a positive example for the future of ocean travel. Find out more about programs and sustainability at SemesterAtSea.org.

Travel Path #4: Studying a Language for Fun

Not in school but still want to learn a language? I recommend looking for a language immersion program that allows you to travel abroad, study a language, and immerse yourself in the culture, usually with a host family.

▶ *Benefits of Language Immersion Programs*

- These programs typically offer you a monthly bundle where you pay a flat fee for food, housing, language classes, and some excursions.
- A program coordination team holds your hand through the process from A to Z.
- More often than not, you live with a host family or a host organization, so you've got people looking out for you.
- You are immersed in the local culture and community, more so than if you just traveled there on your own.

This is a brilliant way to begin your travels in a particular region. When you're living in a local community, you can dive beneath the tourist surface and gain a deeper connection with that culture. Then, when your language immersion program is finished, you leave with the language and tools to travel like a local.

I did this in Bolivia. I lived with a Bolivian family, and my days went like this: I'd go to Spanish classes for a few hours in the morning, volunteer at the botanical garden in the afternoon, then wander the town like I lived there, practicing my Spanish. I'd then go home and have humorously awkward conversations with my host family at dinner, where I'd butcher everything I'd learned in class while eating food I'd never heard of before. It was great. The program organized everything. I just had to show up and put in the effort.

Don't want to commit to a bundled program? Look for language classes once you arrive somewhere. I moved to Bali, rented a house, and once I was settled, signed up for a month of classes at a language school nearby. I studied Bahasa Indonesia five days a week, three hours a day, then was free to go home to my solitary space.

How you choose to study will depend on how much independence you're comfortable having or how much privacy you require because let me tell you that living with a Bolivian mother means that your every move will be monitored as if you were seventeen again...

MOTIVATION: SPENDING MONEY SLOWLY

Travel Path #5: House-Sitting

House-sitting feels like swapping lives with a total stranger in a consensual way. Here's how it works: a homeowner needs to go on a trip, and a house sitter swoops in to take care of the home, pets, and plants while they're away.

I've been a pet sitter in Costa Rica, Mexico, Thailand, and Seattle. I love that house sits are usually low-commitment timewise, ranging anywhere from a weekend to a few months. And with pet sits you get to pretend you have pets while not actually owning pets. It's like being an aunt rather than a mother.

Without the pressure of paying rent, you're able to focus all your time and attention on personal and professional development. Instead of waking up to go to work to pay bills, you're waking up to take the dogs on a walk while contemplating your life choices and returning to a free roof over your head where you have the whole day, week, or month to work on you!

Fun fact: while house-sitting in Mexico, I built my freelance writing career and became a pioneer of the digital nomad movement (more on that later in this chapter). Even funner fact: The Solo Girl's Travel Guide was created during a three-month house sit in the jungles of Thailand. Truthfully, without these house sits and without the emotional support of animals big and small, I may never have gotten to where I am today.

House-sitting is not only a budget-friendly way to travel, but it's also an eco-friendly way to travel. The concept of sharing spaces, places, and pets is something I'd like to see become mainstream.

House-sitting has taken me to towns and neighborhoods I never would have thought to visit. In Costa Rica, I lived in a sprawling mansion in the mountains with views of the ocean, where I could walk to waterfalls. In Thailand, I lived deep in the jungle, where I'd watch my neighbors collect ant eggs from ant nests to make ant egg salad. In Mexico...well, I didn't pick those houses very wisely. One house in particular had no air-conditioning, and drunk construction workers often passed out on my stoop. So please choose carefully before you commit.

Questions to ask to see if a sit is right for you:

♦ How's the wifi?
♦ Will I need a car?
♦ Is the location safe?
♦ Can I walk to grocery stores and markets?

Do everyone a favor and be certain you're up for the challenge. The worst-case scenario for a homeowner is hiring a house sitter who bails halfway through the sit because they came in with unrealistic expectations and underestimated the scope of responsibility.

Furthermore, please understand that house-sitting isn't a "free stay." You are paying rent with your time and effort. This is an exchange. Sitters have responsibilities to take seriously.

▶ *Pet-Sitting*

Before you apply to a sit with a pet, know ...

♦ You must work around that pet's schedule; you can't be away from the house too long.
♦ You can't lose the dog on a walk. Seriously. Ask the pet owner how easy or crazy their pet is before you agree to put their life and leash in your hands.
♦ You've got to feed, pick up after, and love these animals as if they were your own. (Same goes for plants.)

▶ Where to Find House-Sitting Gigs

If you are a responsible human, house-sitting offers you never-ending adventures and animal cuddles across the globe. I love house-sitting so much that I treat my house-sitting app like Tinder. I'm constantly swiping and crushing on new profiles around the world. It's addictive! The website and app I recommend is called TrustedHousesitters. It requires a yearly fee from both the sitter and the homeowner. That fee pays for your background check; plus, I find that a mandatory fee tends to filter out the riffraff. No freeloaders here. Set up a profile and start browsing.

The way I got started with house-sitting, however, was not through this app. I started through Facebook. I'd post my house-sitting résumé in destination-specific expat Facebook groups ("Girls in Spain," for example), and expats who needed a sitter would respond. If you're open to traveling anywhere, look in general house-sitting/pet-sitting Facebook groups. You'll find last-minute house sits needed this weekend and house sits for next year. You can go on a whim or plan in advance!

Pro tip: When applying to a house-sitting opportunity, a pitch that starts with something like "Oh my god! I have always wanted to live in Mexico — I love tacos" will not work. Think about the anxiety a homeowner feels leaving their home or fur baby with a stranger. Your goal is to assure them that you will take care of their home so they can travel worry-free. Homeowners want to know who you are and your motivations, but they also want to know that you'll take this seriously. So take this seriously.

And hey, if you're in the UK or Australia, know that there are so many house-sitting opportunities near you! Tons!

House-Swapping

Own a home? Don't want to sell it or rent it but craving an adventure abroad? Look into house-swapping, where you trade homes with other homeowners around the world. They stay in your home while you stay in theirs. Check out LoveHomeSwap.com.

Travel Path #6: Volunteering

To lend your skills, education, and time to make positive change in the world while traveling is a dream come true. You're doing good while living your life to the fullest! Making a difference while learning about new places and cultures! This is the most rewarding way to travel, and it's how my travel journey began.

Volunteer opportunities and perks depend on how much time you're willing to commit and the skills or education you have to offer.

◆ Some volunteer programs pay for literally everything (flights, housing, food, monthly allowances, and culturally immersive experiences).
◆ Some volunteer positions offer free housing and food.
◆ Some volunteer positions ask for you to pay for your cost of living, including housing and food.

My first one-way ticket was fully paid for by the Peace Corps, an American organization that matches qualified applicants with volunteer assignments; pays for their flights, housing, insurance, and language training; and provides a modest monthly stipend to cover the cost of living. My Peace

Corps assignment sent me to Bulgaria … so now I speak Bulgarian, which, honestly, is not the most useful language out there. But hey, I now know how to read the Cyrillic alphabet and can survive death-defying winters with no central heating (the trick is drinking rakia, which is essentially moonshine). But I digress …

When volunteering with a government organization, you can usually expect some financial support, whereas small, private organizations may not have the budget to fund you, but still need you. And needing you is key.

▶ *Beware of Moneymaking Volunteer Scams*

The dirty truth is that some "volunteer" opportunities in the developing world are actually just money-grabbing businesses masquerading as orphanages or nongovernmental organizations (NGOs) in need. When you pay to volunteer at places like this, instead of helping, you're incentivizing an industry that abuses vulnerable communities. A red flag is any opportunity that allows you to interact with children on a short-term basis and does not require background checks for their volunteers.

Take the "orphanage" industry in Cambodia, for example. Kindhearted tourists and travelers visit Cambodia with good intentions set on helping disadvantaged children, women, and youth. Knowing that there is essentially a market for nice people with big wallets, fake "orphanages" pop up to take advantage. These greedy organizations pose as orphanages, filling their beds with children who have been rented from their families to entertain "voluntourists." The standard estimate is that approximately 70 to 80 percent of these children have at least one parent who is alive, albeit usually quite poor.

The parents are manipulated into sending their children off to orphanages that promise to provide their children with better lives but in reality end up exploiting them.

So, no, many children in these pay-to-play "orphanages" in developing countries are not necessarily orphans. They are more likely rented props living in child zoos for people to come take photos of and then leave.

Places like this don't need you.

You can do a deep dive on this issue by watching a documentary by VICE News called *Cambodia's Fake Orphan Scam* available on YouTube.

My point is that you must be very, very careful when choosing where to volunteer. As a rule of thumb, avoid any organization that offers you the chance to "play with the kids."

Another rule of thumb: Before you volunteer, ask yourself: *Are my skills truly beneficial to this project or community?*

For example, building houses. Do you know anything about building houses? Are there local people who could build these houses better than you? If so, why are you flying to Nicaragua to build houses? I've even heard of build sites where the locals return overnight to undo the terrible work of the volunteers and redo it themselves. You're not helping if you're not skilled to help.

▶ *Finding Good Volunteer Programs*

Sometimes, however, you *will* pay to volunteer, and that money will go toward supporting the organization. That alone does not necessarily mean you're funding a scam. The money you pay may be split between covering your cost of living and training, plus contributing to the honeypot that allows the organization to grow and thrive.

In short, the difference between a good profit and a bad profit all depends on where that money is going.

Bad profit: Goes directly into the pockets of the organizers or managers, rather than benefiting the cause.

Good profit: Goes toward your cost of living, plus paying for the training required to bring you in, plus things the organization needs to keep their program running, like books, gardening tools, or the repairman's salary. Covering or contributing to these costs is okay as long as you're also providing value and aren't just a cash cow.

At the end of the day, the number one goal of both you and the organization should be to benefit the cause.

Here are some questions you can ask a volunteer program to help ensure that they are ethical and a good fit for you.

1. What is the mission of your organization?
2. Are you a registered nonprofit organization? If so, can you provide proof of your nonprofit status?
3. What percentage of your funding goes directly to the programs and projects?
4. Can you provide references or testimonials from past volunteers?
5. What kind of background checks do you conduct on your staff and volunteers?
6. What kind of orientation and training do you provide for volunteers?
7. Can you provide a detailed breakdown of the fees and expenses associated with the program?
8. Are there any hidden costs that volunteers should be aware of?

9. Can you provide a detailed itinerary of the volunteer program and the activities involved?

By asking these questions, you can get a better sense of the organization's legitimacy and the quality of the program they offer.

I've got a list of ethical volunteer opportunities on my website at Alexa-West.com/OneWay that will help you make a positive change in the world while traveling. If you have some opportunities to add to the list, please email me at Alexa@Alexa-West.com.

Travel Path #7: Work-Trade

An economical way to travel without depleting your bank account is to provide a service in exchange for food and accommodations, instead of getting paid in cash.

▶ How to Find Work-Trade Positions

Option 1: Perhaps the most popular and trusted work-exchange platforms are Workaway.com, Worldpackers.com, and WWOOF.net. Go on these websites, and you'll find thousands of exchange opportunities around the world. Here are some common exchanges you'll find:

- ◆ Assisting at an animal shelter
- ◆ Farm and conservation work
- ◆ Helping out at a summer camp
- ◆ Working at a hostel or hotel
- ◆ Doing photography or social media work

Some programs will call this "volunteering," but unless you're contributing to the greater good or some altruistic cause, you're essentially just lending a helping hand, which I consider "work" not volunteering. *Semantics.*

Option 2: Find or create opportunities on your own in the following ways:

Reach out: Find an NGO or small business you admire and contact them directly. Maybe you want to learn about reef restoration, and they need a web designer. See if there's a trade you can make.

Work in a hostel: I worked in hostels in Cambodia and Thailand where my food, drinks, and stay were free. I played many roles: bartender, bed maker, receptionist, therapist. I went months spending just $5 to $10 a day while living the backpacker life.

Hotel photography: Ever see a hotel website with hideous photos? Traveling with a camera or drone? Offer them property photography in exchange for a few nights' stay and food.

Menu translation or design: See a restaurant in Uzbekistan with improper translations or outdated designs? Offer to give their menu a makeover in exchange for a few days of free food.

English lessons for the staff: Hotels and restaurants that want to cater to Western customers can increase their profits by increasing communication. Offer a one- to three-day series of mini–English lessons for the establishments' staff in exchange for room and board.

Always keep an eye out and seize opportunities as they cross your path. The further off the beaten path you are, the more opportunities you may find.

▶ *Things to Know*

◆   Do not ask to get paid! Once you accept money, you're working illegally. Keep this as a trade only.

◆   Many jobs abroad start as volunteer work or internships. If you can convince the boss that you're a huge asset, they may sponsor your visa. And then you can work legally. Congratulations.

MOTIVATION: MAKING MONEY ABROAD

Travel Path #8: Teaching or Working in Education

I've been an ESL teacher in South Korea, Taiwan, and Thailand. But I can also vouch for teaching programs in Japan, Malaysia, Cambodia, Singapore, Hong Kong, the UAE, and Vietnam. All in Asia. Why do I so highly recommend Asia for teachers? Schools in Asia tend to offer the best teaching packages, period.

Each country has its own set of requirements and benefits for teachers, but my favorite teaching destination is South Korea!

▶ *Crash Course for Teaching in South Korea*

Benefits: Your flights, housing, and medical insurance are paid for by your school, so every penny you make is a penny you keep (besides taxes).

Safety: South Korea is one of the safest countries in the world.

Requirements: To teach English in South Korea, you must come from a native English-speaking country, pass a criminal background check, and hold a bachelor's degree in *anything*. If you do not come from a native English-speaking country, look for teaching jobs in Spanish, mathematics, PE (physical education), or art.

How long: One-year contracts.

Private or public? Private schools (called *hagwons*) may pay better but work you harder, whereas the EPIK program (public schools) offers you a more stable schedule and more vacation time. Do some research to see which is a better fit for you.

Do you have a teaching degree or a master's degree? Then congratulations, you qualify to work in the best-paying education-sector jobs and careers anywhere in the world, including international schools, universities, and DoDEA (US Department of Defense Education Activity) schools abroad.

▶ How to Find Teaching Jobs

The number one place to find international teaching jobs is ESLCafe.com, a job board where schools and agencies post teaching positions all over the world.

I applied for my teaching jobs in South Korea when I was physically in the USA. The application to become a teacher in South Korea takes months, so there was no need for me to be in Asia during the application process. I interviewed over the phone. But sometimes, being in the country where you're applying for a teaching position can give you an upper hand. For example, I flew to Taiwan and signed a lease on an apartment before I had a job. Since I was already in town, once I started applying for jobs, I was able to say, "I can come in for an interview tomorrow." I had job offers left and right within a week.

You can also apply directly with schools and departments, rather than looking on job boards. Intent on teaching in Malaysia? If you have a degree in education, getting a job there could be as easy as visiting the website of every international school in Kuala Lumpur and applying for job openings. If you don't have a teaching degree, search for private language schools that accept just bachelor's degrees and send in your résumé, along with when you're hoping to start a teaching job. They may need a teacher soon but haven't yet posted the listing. Get ahead of the game!

Again, I must say that I love ESL and TEFL teacher training programs, where, for example, you study for a month in Vietnam alongside other aspiring ESL/TEFL teachers, and when you complete the training, the program helps you find a teaching job. This is a comfortable way to smoothly transition into living abroad. Check out International TEFL Academy (InternationalTEFLAcademy.com) and International TEFL and TESOL Training (ITTT) (TEFLOnline.net) for in-country programs.

Travel Path #9: Working Holiday Visa

A select number of countries offer this really cool visa where you can legally work while traveling. Countries include Australia, New Zealand, Canada, Japan, the UK, Hong Kong, France, Germany, and beyond! Working holiday visas are usually twelve months but can be extended.

For example, the working holiday visa in Australia is, according to their Department of Home Affairs website, "for young adults who want an extended holiday and to work here to fund it." This visa allows you to legally work and travel in Australia with plenty of time for surfing, socializing, and exploring. And you're not stuck in one place for the entirety of the visa. You can do farmwork harvesting pineapples for a few months, then hop over to the Gold Coast to work in a café for a few months. You can find multiple jobs that fit into one visa allowance.

▶ *Qualifications for the Australian Working Holiday Visa*

◆ Must be between eighteen and thirty years old.
◆ Must prove you have sufficient funds in the bank ($4,000 USD or more).
◆ Must pass a background check and medical check.

How to find jobs: Each country or region has job boards and Facebook groups that list holiday visa jobs. To get an idea of what these jobs look like, start browsing jobs in Australia at BackpackerJobBoard.com.au.

Travel Path #10: Landing a Long-Term Job or Career Abroad

Sometimes, your skills or language are even more valuable in a country other than your own — which makes you a fabulous candidate to land a job abroad. Here are some examples of friends who have found success working overseas.

My American friend Doug has worked for a few airlines, American Express, and now Macquarie (an Aussie investment bank) for over twenty years in the US, Paris, London, and Sydney. Now, he's got his dual citizenship and carries both American and Australian passports.

Carla, a friend from Spain, needed a change, so she took a trip to Bali, began knocking on doors, and landed a job at a Spanish architecture firm on the island.

Her friend Pilar, also from Spain, works for Mastercard and just completed two years working from their Mexico City office.

If you don't want to quit your career, travel with it instead.

▶ *How to Find Jobs Abroad*

◆ Check the job boards of big corporations (such as Disney and American Express).

◆ Check out job boards like Idealist and Indeed World-wide.

◆ If the company you work for now has offices abroad, pull an *Emily in Paris* and see if you can transfer internally to somewhere sexy.

Travel Path #11: Career in the Hospitality, Athletics, or Beauty and Wellness Industry

While writing this book, I stayed at a fancy luxury resort in Siem Reap, Cambodia, run by a GM (general manager) named Ewan from South Africa. Over the past twenty odd years, Ewan has worked his way up in the luxury hotel business in Sri Lanka, Malaysia, Thailand, and now Cambodia. He has even been able to bring his partner along on the journey. Ewan is crushing career goals while traveling the world, but he isn't that unique (no offense, Ewan). In fact, many high-end hotels, restaurants, spas, and bars around the world often hire Western staff when their target market is Western clientele.

Do you work as a waitress now? A hostess? A manager? A GM? A chef? A massage therapist? A bartender? A tennis coach, yoga teacher, or DJ even? You can take this profession overseas.

How to get these jobs: Big hotel or hostel chains like Selina, Marriott, and Four Seasons will post job openings on their website or hire within. A girlfriend of mine had been working in the hotel industry in Ireland for years and wanted a life makeover. She started browsing hotel websites and applying to job openings. She's now the GM of a brand-new resort in the Caribbean.

When I landed my hostel jobs, however, I just showed up on an island, let managers know I was looking for a job, and was hired that very same day. My greatest asset was that I was there. If you can't find jobs online, go knock on doors.

Travel Path #12: Working as a Nanny or Au Pair

Imagine a family in France that wants their kids to grow up speaking English, and so they bring you over, cover your cost of living, and pay you a salary. With the right family, this can be a jackpot opportunity not just for English speakers but for any speakers — German, Chinese, Spanish, whatever.

You do not have to move to France to be a traveling nanny, however. The first time I ever went to Hawaii was with the family I was nannying for in college. Mom wanted to sit by the pool in silence, so she brought me along to run around the resort with the kids. Not a bad gig. There are plenty of families who travel often and want a nanny to come along.

Although I chose to live on campus during college, the family I worked for did offer me the option to be a live-in nanny, where I'd either live at their home or they'd rent an apartment for me to live in near their house. Not all positions offer this, but it can be a bonus. However, being a live-in nanny can also be a burden if you do not set boundaries between work time and your time.

Things to consider: You want a family that respects your space, allows you to live your life outside of working hours, and pays you fairly. Once, a family offered me a live-in position and then told me they'd be paying me just $300 a week for my full-time job, since, you know, they were already putting a roof over my head. How did they expect me to live on $300 a week working full-time? No idea.

Make sure that you negotiate your agreement in the early stages! You do not want to work for a nickel-and-dime family. Been there, done that, not worth it.

Where to find nanny jobs: Do a simple search for "best au pair agencies" or "best nanny agencies," and you'll find sites where you create a profile and contact families, or families will contact you. I prefer websites that require the families to pay a fee and that perform a background check on all au pair candidates. The other option is to sign up with an au pair agency that matches you with a family. These agencies usually represent more well-off families, but just keep in mind that better pay doesn't always mean a more fulfilling job.

MOTIVATION: WORKING ONLINE

This is digital nomad territory. Digital nomads are travelers who move around the world while working from their laptop. To find the best locations for digital nomads, visit NomadList .com. This website ranks destinations based on how suitable they are for workers based on cost, comfort, safety, and more!

Before you assume I'm about to encourage world-scale gentrification or something, keep reading. I strongly believe that as digital nomadism and remote work become the norm, the onus is on us travelers to be cognizant of our impact on local cultures and economies. We've got to shift our impact from pure consumption to contribution, but we'll get to that in a later chapter.

Now, let me tell you how you don't have to work three jobs to afford rent anymore…

Travel Path #13: Working Remotely for a Company

Traveling the world while keeping your salary and benefits is awesome. You can ditch your $3,000 a month apartment in San Diego and instead rent a villa in Bali with a private pool and a housekeeper for a fraction of that cost. You can control your cost of living by selecting where you live. You may also get to keep your pension, 401(k), or whatever else it is that corporate adults enjoy.

▶ *Don't Have a Laptop Job Yet?*

◆ Pitch working remotely to your boss, either for a finite amount of time or indefinitely. However, do consider the time difference when comparing office hours to the daylight hours of your next destination. I have friends who live in Bali and work from 9 PM to 3 AM to co-ordinate with their US jobs' time zone. That wouldn't work for me, but it seems fine for them.

◆ Boss says no? Transition into a job that will support the lifestyle you want to live. Use the "remote work" filter when searching online job boards like LinkedIn, Indeed, FlexJobs, and We Work Remotely.

Want to work remotely and travel with a built-in group of friends? Check out a company called Remote Year (Remote Year.com). With Remote Year, you spend every month in a new city while traveling with a group of fellow remote work-ers. You pay a monthly fee, and Remote Year organizes your housing, flights, adventures, and a bunch of other perks. Don't want to commit to a year? Remote Year offers one- and four-month packages, too. Don't have a remote job yet? Remote Year can help you go remote by coaching you on how to pitch a remote position to your current company and/or helping you find a remote gig online via access to their Remote Year job boards.

Laptop Lifestyle Etiquette

Not all cafés or restaurants want digital nomads who buy one coffee and sit for three hours, taking up precious space. My rule is to buy at least one thing per hour, and if the café is getting full and you've been there a while and there are customers waiting to pay more than you, move along.

That being said, some cafés are delighted to provide a space that's cozy for laptop workers who buy one coffee or treat per hour. Digital nomads bring a lot of business to previously sleepy spots. Nowadays, you can also find official coworking spaces and coworking cafés designed to cater to online workers. Official coworking spaces act like offices, with desks, meeting rooms, and soundproof booths for streamers. You can pay hourly or get a membership while you're in town.

Bonus: Coworking spaces are also a great place to meet other online workers!

Travel Path #14: Becoming a Freelancer

I quit my teaching job and started my digital nomad career by writing how-to articles for online dating websites and a doomsday prepper blog. I then studied copywriting on my own and eventually became a pro at writing Amazon sales pages by studying up on the Amazon algorithm. I found a few niches I liked and dove into making myself an authority in copywriting for those niches. I was able to raise my rates quickly and was turning down jobs left and right, instead of looking for them.

You can freelance in many things online: photo and video editing, translating, blog writing, social media marketing, public relations — you name it.

Where to find these gigs: Start on Upwork.com and Fiverr.com.

Pro tip: I took my first few jobs for very low rates — like $5 per gig — just to get a few good reviews on my profile to start attracting clients.

Travel Path #15: Building an Agency

Once you get very good at what you do and develop a reputation or web presence, you no longer have to go looking for clients — they come looking for you. For example, my business partner (and best friend), Emilia, started a graphic design agency where she created logos, labels, and branding for businesses big and small. She was in high demand and was able to travel the world while doing her job. (That's how we met, by the way — while she was in Bali working remotely.)

The benefits: You can set your own prices.

The downside: Owning your own business can mean working long hours.

The upside: You can give yourself breaks between gigs and work from anywhere.

How to start: Begin as a freelancer, build a portfolio, brand yourself with a website where you offer your services, and direct your recurring customers there ... in a nutshell.

Top tip to attract clients: I am much more likely to hire someone after they have taught me something — whether that's through a tutorial on YouTube or useful advice on their blog. Once they've proven their expertise and provided me with value, I want more of it — and I will pay for it. Offer free resources on your website or social media.

Travel Path #16:
Creating a Brand and Monetizing It

I used to hate hearing the word *brand* — especially after living in Bali. Everyone has a freaking brand, and it's usually a girl on Instagram who takes a lot of photos of her butt and uses words like *positivity* and *manifest*...although I totally use those words now. (*Thanks, Bali.*) While I'm not passionate enough about my butt to make a brand out of it, some people do make some serious cash off their butts, which is proof that you can do anything online to make money these days. Kim Kardashian's butt has changed my life. Skims are the only underwear I wear now. *Don't judge me until you try them.* Just like Kim K., when you have a loyal audience (or even a hostile audience that mocks you but secretly wants to be you), your distribution channels are built in. People trust you, and so they want to buy from you.

I no longer roll my eyes at the concept of a personal brand. I encourage it...especially if it has nothing to do with your butt.

Do you get what I'm saying? People want personal. If you can find something that you can talk passionately about every day for the next ten years, then you've got a brand. You can package it, you can sell it, and you can wake up to do something with it every day. The more niche, the better.

A BIG *however*: Do not expect your brand to financially support you overnight, and do not create a brand because you're hoping to become the next Kim K. (although you could be). Brands are businesses. Businesses grow and fail and grow and fail. It takes time. It took me three years to grow The Solo Girl's Travel Guide into a self-sustaining business, but I loved what I was doing so much that I was willing to keep pushing.

I, however, am not the person to teach you about how to create a personal brand and monetize it, but I do have two gurus that I learn from:

Christina Galbato — blogging and social media genius at ChristinaGalbato.com. She left her windowless cubicle to grow her blog and Instagram into a thriving business — and now she teaches others how to do the same. I'm enrolled in her courses on blogging, influencer marketing, and online course creation.

Christian LeBlanc — photographer and vlogger at LostLeBlanc.com. He's a former accountant turned seven-figure content creator. I'm enrolled in his Lost Creator Academy, which is an online course that teaches anybody how to pick up a camera and create a business with it.

These two will teach you the *how*; travel is going to teach you the *what*. Travel is going to help you figure out what problem you want to solve, what lesson you want to teach, or what whimsy you want to spread.

...And this is where I'm going to stop on the never-ending topic of Travel Paths.

Have I inspired you or overwhelmed you? You thought you had no options, and now you know that the world is full of opportunities waiting for you.

Are you going to put this book on a shelf and become painfully indecisive for the next year, or are you going to pick a path and go for it? I think you should go for it.

▶ The Two Ways to Pick Your First Travel Path

1. Get excited about everything, apply to a bunch of opportunities, and see what sticks.
2. Pick one thing and commit.

Both work. You've just got to make that first move.

The chart on the next page shows exactly how my travel path began and evolved. And for comparison, after that is a chart showing how my bestie, Emilia, did it.

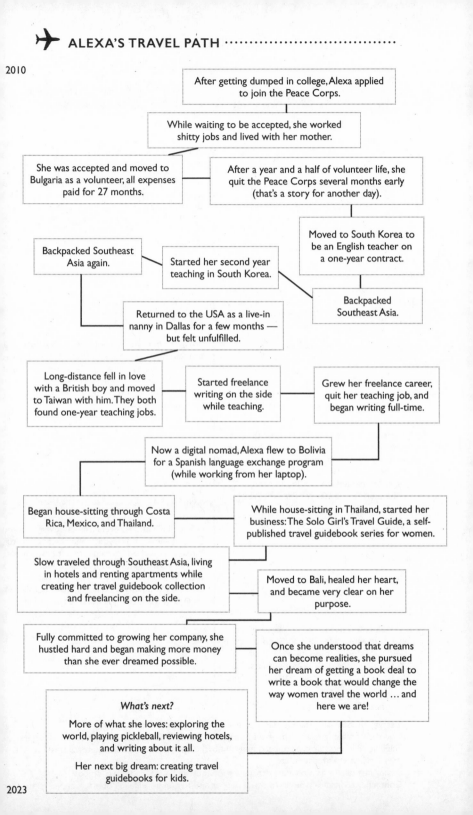

✈ ALEXA'S TRAVEL PATH

2010

After getting dumped in college, Alexa applied to join the Peace Corps.

While waiting to be accepted, she worked shitty jobs and lived with her mother.

She was accepted and moved to Bulgaria as a volunteer, all expenses paid for 27 months.

After a year and a half of volunteer life, she quit the Peace Corps several months early (that's a story for another day).

Moved to South Korea to be an English teacher on a one-year contract.

Backpacked Southeast Asia.

Started her second year teaching in South Korea.

Backpacked Southeast Asia again.

Returned to the USA as a live-in nanny in Dallas for a few months — but felt unfulfilled.

Long-distance fell in love with a British boy and moved to Taiwan with him. They both found one-year teaching jobs.

Started freelance writing on the side while teaching.

Grew her freelance career, quit her teaching job, and began writing full-time.

Now a digital nomad, Alexa flew to Bolivia for a Spanish language exchange program (while working from her laptop).

Began house-sitting through Costa Rica, Mexico, and Thailand.

While house-sitting in Thailand, started her business: The Solo Girl's Travel Guide, a self-published travel guidebook series for women.

Slow traveled through Southeast Asia, living in hotels and renting apartments while creating her travel guidebook collection and freelancing on the side.

Moved to Bali, healed her heart, and became very clear on her purpose.

Fully committed to growing her company, she hustled hard and began making more money than she ever dreamed possible.

Once she understood that dreams can become realities, she pursued her dream of getting a book deal to write a book that would change the way women travel the world … and here we are!

What's next?

More of what she loves: exploring the world, playing pickleball, reviewing hotels, and writing about it all.

Her next big dream: creating travel guidebooks for kids.

2023

✈ EMILIA'S TRAVEL PATH ·····································

1990s

As a child, Emilia dreamed of being an explorer and *National Geographic* photographer.

2013

Began working as a freelance graphic designer while in university.

2015

After graduating from university, went on a two-week marine wildlife conservation expedition with a nonprofit organization to Baja Sur, Mexico. The organization then invited her to work for six weeks in the Peruvian jungle, where she rowed along the Amazon River, worked with local communities, and fell in love with the art of photojournalism.

2016

Moved to La Paz, Baja Sur, to work for that same nonprofit for six more months until the organization went belly-up. Moved back home to Mazatlán, feeling defeated.

2017–2019

Living at home with her parents, Emilia opened an online design agency with a friend. She was then happy in work but unhappy in her personal life at home. She moved into her own apartment, setting aside her dream of traveling the world because that "wasn't realistic."

2019

As her reputation grew, she was invited to work on a project with traditional Mexican artisans. It proved to be a sensational project but a highly toxic work environment that drained her of all joy. She realized she needed to escape this situation and rediscover her creative soul.

2020

Left for Bali for a six-week self-discovery mission carrying Alexa's travel guide. She reached out to Alexa; they met and became instant best friends. Emilia pitched some design ideas to Alexa and soon was officially invited to join The Solo Girl's Travel Guide team. Suddenly, Emilia's talent of design and dreams of travel as a job became her real life.

2022

On a book-research road trip in Baja Sur, Emilia fell in love with a Spanish man. Soon after, she moved to Spain. In Spain, Emilia is pursuing her passions: photography, photojournalism, and creative consulting.

What's next? ··········

- Getting her Spanish residency (and even a Spanish passport in a few years).
- Cocreating travel guides throughout Europe for The Solo Girl's Travel Guide European series.
- Fulfilling childhood dreams of becoming a published photojournalist and editorial travel writer. *(Hey NatGeo, she's ready for you.)*
- Scaling her talents as a creative consultant for tourism boards and travel brands.
- Continuing to inspire women to travel deeper and to pursue a life full of magic and passion.

As you can see, Emilia's travel flow chart is very different (and less chaotic) than mine. I had no idea what I was doing; I made it all up as I went, whereas Emilia had a vision. She used her talents as a photographer and designer to travel and explore and grow her career. Still, she and I both ended up at the same spot in life, living and working together, which goes to show that your path will take you where you're supposed to go, no matter how planned or unplanned it may be. Don't obsess over the details; fall in love with the big picture.

Your path doesn't have to look like either of ours, or you can copy our paths as much as you please!

Homework to Make This Real Life

When you're ready, let's design your dream travel flow chart. It's like a vision board with a timeline! You must dream it before you can have it! Meet me on my website at Alexa-West .com/OneWay to download your free Travel Path template and access complete guides to each Travel Path.

Now that you've got all the opportunities to travel the world by yourself, are you going to sit around for twenty years waiting for someone to go with you? Or are you going to do the bravest things you've ever done and take a big leap of faith alone?

No matter what your answer is right now, I want you to read the next chapter with an open mind ...

CHAPTER 3

The Power of Solo Travel

When my friend Molly video-called me from Bali in tears, I thought someone had died. Turns out, her best friend was supposed to join her on the island, but when she arrived at the airport, she wasn't allowed to board the flight because her passport was going to expire within six months (that's a rule). Consequently, Molly was sobbing and saying, "I don't want to do this alone!" to which I responded, "Molly, the Universe clearly wants you to be alone, since you're so afraid of being alone. Trust the lesson!" Fast-forward a couple days, and these are the messages I began receiving from Molly:

> Oh my god, I want to live here.
> I met a boy. We kissed on his scooter.
> I'm canceling my flight so I can stay longer.
> I've made a friend. She invited me to be her roommate.

Within one week, Molly went from being terrified that she'd be alone forever to falling in love, building a social circle, and moving to Bali.

She thought if she went alone, she'd remain alone. But that's just not true.

✈ **TRAVEL LESSON #3** ·······································

Solo travel does not mean traveling alone.

··

If your friend cancels her trip with you, go anyway. You will meet other solo travelers looking for friends. If you want to teach English in South Korea, go alone. You will meet other teachers. If you want to quit your job and become a freelance writer, go alone. You'll run into other nomads working from their laptops, too. Your people are waiting for you — you just haven't met them yet.

I get it, though. The idea of taking that initial leap alone is scary. We don't have to pretend it's not. It feels much more comfortable to travel with a friend, or really anyone if you're desperate enough to go but don't want to go alone. Just knowing you have someone next to you if things go wrong is ultra-comforting…until it becomes ultra-annoying. Here's a truth you need to know…

THE REALITY OF TRAVELING WITH FRIENDS VS. TRAVELING SOLO

Let's say you want to go to Greece. You're scared to go to Greece alone, so you start asking friends and coworkers if they want to go with you. You even ask your hippie cousin who wears socks with sandals because the thought of being alone in Greece is overwhelming and you're desperate.

So you continue to ask around and terrific news! Your coworker Ashley says she'll come with you! Yay, you like Ashley. You like working with Ashley. You like drinking with Ashley. Ashley has been to Iceland. That's cool. But what you don't realize is that there's a 70 percent probability that Ashley sucks at travel or at least Ashley's style of travel does not match yours. You're an optimist, though, so you and Ashley are going to Greece!

Fast-forward to airport day. You're both ecstatic to be sharing this experience together! But on the plane you encounter your first hiccup: Ashley doesn't want the middle seat even though she was assigned the middle seat. Fine. You compromise and switch with her. You're uncomfortable, but you survive. Then you land. Excited again! Your trip begins.

Day 1: Ashley wants to sit by the pool, and you want to explore. You compromise.

Day 2: You want to eat at a local spot, but she wants the fancy beach club with expensive oysters. You compromise again.

Day 3: You meet a really cool group of people from Argentina who invite you to go dancing with them, but Ashley wants to go back to the hotel. You compromise.

Then you start to resent Ashley. Now that you're safely on the ground in Greece and realize that *hey, this place isn't so scary,* you don't need Ashley. In fact, you wish Ashley never came. She's holding you back from going with the flow and seizing exciting opportunities. This is no longer your trip. This trip has been hijacked by freakin' Ashley. (PS. Sorry to every girl named Ashley. This isn't personal. Love your name.)

In my first two to three years of travel, I made this mistake over and over again. Inviting the Ashleys of the world on trips because I was too nervous to take that first step alone. But after years of solo travel, here's what I've learned: Pre-travel anxiety is worse than actual travel anxiety. Preparing to travel is usually scarier than actually traveling. You feel like you need a travel partner before you go, but once you're out in the world, that anxiety melts away. You make friends as you go and you realize that you totally could have done this on your own!

When you travel solo, you are completely free to do whatever you want. Want to cancel your plans because you were invited to a Brazilian wedding? You can do that! Want to skip your temple tour to stay in bed with a hot guy you met last night? You can do that, too. Want to slow down, rent an apartment in Istanbul, and work for a month? You can certainly do that.

When you are traveling solo, every single decision you make is completely up to you. But when you bring a friend, nearly every single decision is a compromise. You're basically travel-marrying that person (or people) for the duration of your trip. You'll need to consider their needs, moods, and desires just as much as you consider your own.

To travel solo, however, is to be totally selfish. And how many chances are you going to get to be totally selfish in life? Maybe you'll have a family one day, or maybe you'll create a company with ten thousand employees. In any case, people will need you. You can't just disappear into the woods and turn your phone off for a week. The more your life develops, the less opportunity you will have to unplug without a care in the world. So if you've got the opportunity to go alone now, take it and run... but run alone.

So yes, I am trying to convince you to travel solo if only to experience what it feels like to be totally selfish at least once in your life. But I also know that eventually you will travel with a friend, so...

Cheat Sheet: How to Travel with a Friend from Home

Just because you're fabulous friends at home doesn't mean you'll be fabulous travel friends. (The same goes for romantic partners). So here's what you need to do before your trip to keep from killing each other:

❏ Brainstorm and visualize the trip together
❏ Agree on a daily budget
❏ Make bucket lists together (all the things you want to see and do on this trip)
❏ Involve each other in the planning so you're both to blame when something goes wrong
❏ Plan mini-solos (more about this in a sec)

There is a chance that you and your friend will have a magnificent time and plan a million more trips together. In that case, congratulations on finding your travel BFF! Travel BFFs are rare, and it is a cosmic gift when you find the right person to share the world with.

My travel BFF is the incredible Emilia Igartua. She's not only one of my favorite human beings on this planet, but she's also a dream travel partner. Yes, she gets frustrated when I leave wet towels on the floor, and I get frustrated when she... actually, I can't think of anything she does that annoys me while traveling. She's my travel unicorn. But still, even Emilia and I see the value in solo travel and so, when we go on trips together, we like to take a few nights or weeks to have our own solo expeditions. These are called mini-solos.

MINI-SOLOS: EVERYTHING YOU NEED TO KNOW

A mini-solo is when you travel with companions but break off for a night or few days to have a mini-vacation alone.

Let's illustrate this concept with a story from my editor, Kristen:

> *My husband, in the early '90s (way before cellphones and even email), did an around-the-world trip with a friend. They hitchhiked for some of it. When they needed a break from each other, they'd wake up and decide they would each hitch to the next place on their own, so they'd say, for example, 'See you tonight in Queensland at the XYZ Hostel.' Or else they would show up together in a new town and do a mini-solo for the first day. This gave them the experience of discovering things on their own, without compromise or negotiation, and being able to exchange stories when they reunited.*

Get the idea?

▶ Rules of a Mini-Solo

- ◆ In my experience, three nights is the minimum time required to unplug and reconnect with yourself. If you can give yourself three nights alone, that is ideal. But take what you can get, whether that be an afternoon solo or one-month solo.
- ◆ You must be far enough away from each other that it doesn't make sense to eat breakfast, lunch, or dinner together.
- ◆ Limit your contact to just a couple quick calls and short texts. The goal is to detach from your comfort people and hang out with yourself.
- ◆ You may invite each other to eat one meal at a cool place you've found on your own, but only once every forty-eight hours!
- ◆ If you decide you're bored, you're not allowed to call your travel BFF to come save you from boredom. That

defeats the whole purpose of the mini-solo. Your mission is to go inward. Use your boredom as a catalyst to be creative. Be awkward on your own. Meet new people on your own. Figure shit out on your own!

Benefits of a mini-solo: You have someone nearby to bail you out of jail if need be. So take some risks during your mini-solo. Be bold.

When you reunite, you'll be super excited to share stories, show each other new discoveries, and just have your buddy back. Any tension or staleness that was building up before will now be gone, and you'll be eager to continue the mission together!

So if you're not ready to travel alone, travel with your person but schedule some alone time! Introduce the idea before the trip so that your travel buddy won't be blindsided or offended.

EXPERIMENT WITH YOUR ALONE TIME

The cool thing about being on the other side of the world away from everyone who knows you is that…no one knows you. You can be whoever you want when you travel alone, including wonderfully authentic versions of yourself that you just haven't had the opportunity to meet yet.

As you travel, these repressed versions are released depending on the environment: island you, city you, Spanish-speaking you, secretly-eating-meat-even-though-you're-a-vegan you. These are all parts of you, and without judgment, you can let them out to play! You can explore new sides to your personality, sexuality, sense of fashion, and spirituality. Whatever feels good, you can follow. As time goes on, you'll still be you, just the all-embracing version of you who has stepped into her full potential.

Consciously or subconsciously, you've been following the rules of your family, society, and community since you learned how to walk. But not out here. Those little expectations to be who you've always been don't exist. You can break character. The role you play back home is not the role you're expected to play when you travel solo.

But usually, you can't do that if you bring a friend along, no matter how open-minded you think they are. If you bring a friend, you're bringing those conscious or unconscious social constructs with you. Whether you intend to or not, when you look at your friend you will be looking into a mirror from home — and that's not the point of this trip. The point is to break the mirror and see yourself from a different angle.

You won't fully feel what I'm talking about until you're eating pizza alone in Italy, becoming a surfer chick in Mexico, or on a wilderness expedition in Alaska sleeping under the stars. But when you're there, you'll think back to what you're reading right now and understand that you've shed skin you never realized you were wearing. You'll feel new, but this is just the real you, uncovered.

Mini Writing Exercise

Write down or simply ponder three elements of your personality that you want to explore more. Is it dressing like your role model? Is it experimenting with your sexuality or your posture, speaking more slowly, being more active, trying sobriety, going vegetarian, going un-vegetarian? This is your chance to totally focus on developing yourself without judgment.

BUT ISN'T TRAVELING ALONE DANGEROUS?

Um, if you throw a random dart at a map and just turn up without any research whatsoever, then yes, solo travel can be dangerous. So can turning down the wrong alley in New York or wandering into the Amazon rainforest without a guide. But you're not doing any of that. In fact, nearly everywhere you go as a traveler, you've made an informed choice to go.

Travel to Safer Destinations

Would I wander the dark streets of Seattle (where I currently live half the year) alone at night? No, no, I would not. Would I wander the well-lit, busy night markets of Seoul alone until 2 AM and then go eat deep-fried squid on a stick and buy a beer from a minimart and sit and watch the street performers and skateboarders? Sure would, will, and do.

When I tell you that I feel safer traveling than I do at home, I mean it. This is because I choose my locations based on safety. If you come from a high-crime city, then you are safer from random crime or assault when you travel to a lower-crime city. Makes sense, right? You are placing yourself in safer places.

So, for me, traveling from Seattle to Seoul actually puts me in a safer environment. I don't have to worry about gun violence, fentanyl addicts, or robberies as severely as I do in Seattle. While I still need to use street smarts, I know that Seoul is extremely safe. I may still be a little nervous to travel to Seoul, but there's a difference between being scared and being nervous. *Scared* is about fear, whereas *nervous* is about anticipation of the unknown. Choose destinations that make you nervous, not ones that make you scared.

Approved Destinations for Solo Female Travelers

I update my list of the best travel destinations for girls every year on my website. Visit Alexa-West.com/OneWay to find where I recommend you visit and avoid based on safety (and comfort and nature and food).

Before I hit up a new city, I check that destination's crime index on Numbeo.com/crime and its safety rating on NomadList.com. I learn which risks to be aware of and how to prepare for them. In chapter 6, we will discuss safety in depth, so for the moment, let's toss the danger thing aside. Instead, I want to tell you how wonderful and healing the world is. How it's filled with good people who will treat you like their daughter. How you are being called to follow that little voice inside you that's pulling you into the unknown. How traveling alone isn't as scary as it sounds.

At the end of the day, this trip is about you falling in love with yourself. When you find yourself alone, don't fight it or wish it away. Be the girl who can go to dinner alone, take a walk alone, and admire herself alone. No one can ever take you away from you. There's power in that.

Homework Challenge

Does the idea of going alone make you really nervous? Start with small solo outings at home. Take yourself out on a self-date. Go out to dinner, go to a movie, or simply start with going for a walk and getting some ice cream by yourself. Start imagining yourself wandering the colorful streets of Havana instead of your local park. How does that feel? Exciting? Freeing? Petrifying? Stay with that feeling. Any time you feel nervous, replace that nervousness with fascination and let excitement win.

Thousands of women travel alone every day. If they can do it, so can you!

Mantra: Today I will replace fear with curiosity.

CHAPTER 4

Travel Is Rescue

Want to hear something crazy about my family? I have two older brothers, and they both live in Asia. Joey moved to Taiwan after college to get his master's degree and study Mandarin. Fifteen years later, he's still in Asia, now with a wife and two kids. My brother Brady moved to Thailand about seven years ago, dove into the Brazilian jiujitsu world, and started a business. Brady speaks Thai. Joey speaks Mandarin, Japanese, and Korean. To all three of us, living abroad is normal.

Whenever I tell someone that both my brothers also live in Asia, they ask me if we planned it together. The answer is no. We may have been subliminally inspired by each other, but each of us chose to leave the States and move to Asia independently.

Joey left because he wanted to study and immerse himself in Asian culture. Brady left because his job at home was unfulfilling, and just two weeks of vacation time per year is ridiculous. And I left because I wanted something better than what I grew up with. Our father wasn't too interested in being a father, and our mother drank a lot of wine in the basement and brought a new boyfriend into the picture every six months. Since I was old enough to collect my own babysitting money,

I wanted to get the fuck out of there. (My therapist says there are much deeper reasons for us leaving than just these, but we'll save that for the next book.)

For my siblings and me, I say travel was rescue. Travel was and is an opportunity for us to choose what we want for our lives rather than accepting what was decided for us by our family and society.

My mother once insinuated that my brothers and I were running away from whatever life she thought we should be living, and I only partially disagree. While it might be true that we didn't turn out to be good little 9-to-5 office workers with mortgages and midtwenties marriages like she had hoped, we didn't run away from that. We walked away. "Running away" suggests that you're avoiding a challenge or fleeing a crime scene. Walking away, however, is when you have enough courage to say no to something that doesn't serve you and decide to choose better. Walking away is powerful.

So what is it time for you to walk away from?

Maybe it's something huge, like a relationship or a job that you know is a total waste of time. Maybe you need to get real and walk away from a toxic version of yourself (we've all got a little toxic princess inside us that needs to be put in her place so we can establish healthier coping mechanisms). Or maybe you're like, "God, I just want to go travel the world, lie on beautiful beaches, and drink margaritas! Enough with this therapist shit." But trust me when I tell you that when you're sitting on that beach, away from the distractions of your normal reality, you'll begin to identify parts of your life that you want to change. You'll begin to realize that you wish your day-to-day life felt like this. More exciting, more fulfilling, less stress, less bullshit. You'll begin to realize that there are some people in your social circle that you're better off without. Most likely, you'll also come to the realization that you need to start treating yourself better and stop with the negative self-talk because life is meant to be enjoyed.

Clarity comes with detachment. Do not waste clarity. Do not ignore it. You must be ready to take that clarity and turn it into action on the other side of the world. Travel is therapy, so let's get started on this therapist shit now.

✈ **TRAVEL LESSON #4** ·······································

Before every trip, set an intention.

···

This intention is what transforms an indulgent vacation into a mission of self-exploration. Rather than flopping on a beach to get drunk, you're flopping on a beach to get clarity, solve a puzzle, or heal a wound…and maybe to also get a little drunk. When you return home or move on to the next destination, you will have met that intention and leveled up.

With each new destination, set a new intention and watch yourself grow.

Setting Your Intention

To find your intention, ask yourself this: *What's missing?* Or *What do I want to let go of?*

Is something missing in your love life, bank account, emotional tank? Do you need to walk away from unhealthy patterns or people? Ask yourself, *What's missing?* or *What do I need to let go of?* and run with the first thing that comes to mind.

Then set an intention to address whatever is going on, and carry it with you. Here are some examples that you can borrow and use, if you'd like.

What's missing? Self-confidence.
Intention: To keep a journal and write down every time I get a compliment or someone says something nice about me. To give myself compliments and write down my accomplishments each day.

What do I want to let go of? Drinking too much.
Intention: To limit myself to one drink per day and replace my other drinks with spritzers or healthy elixirs.

What's missing? Feeling alive.
Intention: To do things outside my comfort zone.

What do I want to let go of? My toxic family that belittles me, gaslights me, and makes me feel like I'll never be anything special.
Intention: To reflect on what or who hurts me and set clear boundaries to finally live my life on my terms.

What's missing? A romantic partner.
Intention: To date. To set healthy standards of what I want in a partner and uphold them while I put myself in romantic situations.

What do I want to let go of? Terrible spending habits.
Intention: To set a daily budget for myself, use a budgeting app, and practice discipline in my spending.

Your intentions don't have to be cataclysmic, but over time, they will have a cataclysmic effect on your quality of life. Setting and fulfilling these intentions is how you transform vacation travel into Glow Up Travel™. *Yes, I trademarked my girls-only trips as Glow Up Travel because this equation works:*

Intention + Travel = Glowing and Growing

Whatever you decide is missing or whatever it is that you need to walk away from, you can layer it on top of all the fun you're going to have on your trip. Your intentions will be the background music that plays in your mind while you're getting a massage on the beach, volunteering at an animal shelter, or lying in a hammock by the river.

Speaking of background music, this book has a playlist for your travels! Go to Alexa-West.com/OneWay.

I know you're not traveling just to take photos in pretty dresses. *Thank goodness that era is coming to an end.* There's something big you need to let go of, even if you're not aware of it yet. Figure it out before you go. Or at least be ready for when it falls on your lap while you're sitting on the beach.

When you're planning your getaway, this intention is what will get you through the doubt, fear, and hesitation of going. Instead of seeing this trip as a selfish vacation, you'll see it as therapy and personal development with vacation undertones.

The fact that you're reading this book is no coincidence. It's a sign (you'll believe in those soon) that something bigger or more magical is waiting for you. If you feel like you're not where you're supposed to be, you're not where you're supposed to be. If you feel like something is missing, something is missing. Don't ignore that feeling. Listen to it. Don't make this complicated. It's your turn to be happy.

PART TWO

SURVIVING AND THRIVING

As you'll see next, we're not getting into the nitty-gritty of trip planning just yet.

Why? Because that's the easy part. The ambitious part is envisioning yourself in a foreign country, speaking foreign languages, making new friends, and feeling like you're exactly where you're meant to be.

Preparing your soul and expectations comes first. Then, in part 3, we'll get into the logistics of packing, leaving, and landing.

CHAPTER 5

Culture and Shock

Did you know that in India, people bob their heads side to side to communicate "yes, I agree" or "that's correct"?

Did you know that in Thailand, it is common to use a spoon and fork instead of chopsticks when eating? The fork is used to push food onto the spoon, which is then brought to the mouth.

Did you know that in Pakistan, India, and many Muslim countries your right hand is used for eating and greeting, and your left hand is used for bathroom hygiene?

And did you know that in many developing countries, you don't flush your toilet paper? The septic systems can't handle it. Instead, there will be a bin for you to throw your used toilet paper in.

Welcome to the chapter full of weird stuff no one tells you about!

I'm going to be filling you in on the little things that travelers usually learn through uncomfortable encounters, strange situations, and middle-of-the-night mistakes — and how to handle them.

When I think of the most awkward cultural mistakes I've made, here's what comes to mind:

- Trying to hug a monk in Thailand. No one is allowed to touch a monk. Not you, not me, not Oprah.
- Entering a temple in Bali while on my period. It is forbidden for women to enter a temple while menstruating because the Balinese (as well as other Buddhist or Hindu cultures) believe that your blood is impure, will dirty the temple, and will make the spirits angry.
- Stirring wasabi into my soy sauce in Tokyo. You're supposed to put a tiny piece of wasabi on top of your sushi and then delicately dip your sushi into some soy sauce, rather than dunking it. It's an insult to the chef to smother his creation.

In all these instances, I could have died of embarrassment, but instead I decided to evoke...

✈ **TRAVEL LESSON #5** ···

Humor is a travel survival skill.

···

The bravest travelers I know all have one thing in common: They can laugh at themselves. They aren't shy about making mistakes, and they are okay when someone laughs at their mistakes.

You always have a choice to face cultural misunderstandings either with anger, with embarrassment, or with humor. You already look different and act strangely. People are not going to expect you to know exactly what to do the first time you eat bún chả in Vietnam or attend a wedding in Nigeria. Embrace being the weirdo who needs help. Asking for help garners human connection! People love to help!

What you shouldn't do is not try something because you're afraid to look stupid. That's stupid!

If you are about to enter a situation where you have no clue what you're doing, ask for guidance before you try. But try!

CULTURE SHOCK

No matter where you go, you're going to encounter little cultural nuances that you've never experienced before. Encountering these nuances too quickly or all at once is called culture shock. Culture shock is best described as a feeling of being overwhelmed or disoriented by social norms or attitudes that suddenly surround you.

When you resist understanding or continue to compare a foreign culture to your own, culture shock feels impossible to overcome. On the other hand, if you can stay open, curious, and inquisitive, you can turn culture shock into culture awe.

To minimize culture shock, study cultural customs and faux pas for the destination you're visiting before you go. Going to Japan? Just go on YouTube, search for "cultural customs in Japan," and brief yourself on what to expect. When you land in Japan, instead of being confused and nervous your first time in a ryokan (traditional inn), you make a game of spotting and participating in cultural norms like bowing when you greet your host and taking your shoes off before you enter.

With that said, watching a YouTube video, reading books, and asking your Japanese friend for some pointers will certainly help you, but they can't prepare you for every single cultural encounter. So let's prepare for the things you can't prepare for.

Food You Don't Want to Eat

I was served cow tongue in Bolivia. I was living with a host family while studying Spanish, and I'd eat dinner with them every night. I ate a lot of unpleasant things, like watery flan, rubbery chicken, and bland mystery soups. To this day, I don't know if I don't like Bolivian food or if my host mother was just a really bad cook. But one day, an entire cow tongue, taste buds and all, was flopped on my plate. Pale pink, boiled, no flavor, just texture! That was the most dreadful meal of my life. I ate small bites and "filled up" on the side dishes while cutting the tongue into tiny pieces and burying it under things.

One of the rudest things you can do in some cultures is refuse food that is served to you, especially when it's one of those "guest of honor delicacies" like fish eyeballs! So what do you do when you really, really don't want to eat something?

Option 1: Simply be honest that you're not ready to eat that far outside your comfort zone. A sincere "thank you, but no thank you."

Option 2: Take small bites and fill up on the side dishes. Chase your bites with alcohol. Swallow what you can. It'll make for a good story.

Option 3: When the situation calls for it, say you're vegetarian. I am a carnivore. I love meat, but I love familiar parts of meat. I don't love tendons, intestines, or organs. So, when I think I am about to be served unidentifiable meat, I ask for a vegetarian option. I usually do this when I'm eating at someone's home and don't want to be rude, but I also do this at restaurants. If I'm not confident in the menu, I order vegetarian dishes. Or if that country's cuisine scares me, I'll eat at vegetarian restaurants. Removing the meat removes the mystery.

I mix and match these methods depending on the setting.

In Bulgaria, while living with my Peace Corps host family, I was eating things I didn't like on a daily basis because I wasn't going to be the princess who demanded that an entire family start cooking special meals just to accommodate me. However, I did use positive reinforcement, telling them when I genuinely did like something. Soon, I started coming home to more fresh veggies and less mystery meat.

Also important: Do you have a food allergy? If so, definitely communicate that loud and clear. You should also know that many restaurant kitchens around the world are not trained to handle food allergies. For example, if you say, "no shrimp," your food might very well come with no shrimp, but the kitchen might not understand the concept of cross-contamination, so if there is shrimp in that kitchen, there is a chance your lettuce has touched the knife or the cutting board or the container with the shrimp! Or fish sauce! The thing about fish sauce is that it is often made with shrimp shells, but maybe the young chef doesn't know that. And did you know that in many cultures, fish sauce is used to flavor even nonseafood dishes? Such as *pad krapow moo* (stir-fried pork with basil) in Thailand. So if your allergies are severe, a better question to ask is "Do you cook shrimp in that kitchen?" If the answer is yes, depending on the sophistication of the kitchen or restaurant and your ability to communicate the severity of your allergy, you might want to altogether avoid the restaurant.

Pro Food Tip

When I go to Emilia's house in Mexico and eat at the table with her family, I often wait to see how they go about eating dishes I'm not familiar with, and then copy what they do. Are they eating with their hands? Are they dipping their food in the salsa or drizzling salsa on top? Watch, learn, eat.

However, in some cultures, if you're the guest of honor, you eat first. If you don't know how to eat what you're eating, don't be afraid to say so! Again, humor is your friend.

People Asking Personal Questions

"Have you eaten breakfast?"

"Where are you going?"

"How much money do you make?"

"Are you married?"

"Are you alone?"

In some cultures, these questions might be totally appropriate, or they might be totally creepy. It's hard to know! Sometimes I answer these questions truthfully, sometimes I keep my answers vague, and sometimes I straight-up lie.

You'll soon learn that in some cultures, there's a thin line between love and friendship. You may think you're just being friendly, but your taxi driver might think you're in love with him. With men, I usually keep my conversation guard up until I trust them. I'll tell them my husband is waiting for me at the restaurant, and I'll even go so far as having a fake conversation on my phone. "Hi, babe. I'll be there in five minutes. Love you, too!" I want my taxi driver or host to know that there is no chance of marriage between us. Have no shame in your safety game.

Sidenote: If you follow me on Instagram, you probably know that I'm extremely close with my team of drivers in Bali. They started as strangers but have turned into my surrogate brothers and dads. I've met their kids, eaten in their homes, and consider them family. But we had to earn each other's trust over time. Start guarded with the hopes of opening up and letting people in.

Language Barriers

I speak six languages... but in five of them, my proficiency is just that of a feisty four-year-old. I am able to order food, give compliments, haggle in markets, show gratitude, and ask very simple questions. But you wouldn't believe the power that comes with being able to speak Indonesian like a four-year-old! I get more smiles, better prices, special treatment, friendship, connection, and most importantly, homemade whiskey from farmers. I also get ripped off way less than the other tourists who point and yell, "Yes, hello! HOW MUCH IS THAT?!"

If you can learn to count to ten (easier than you think) and learn a collection of fifteen common phrases, you will unlock new levels of travel wherever you go. Take a little time to study even the most basic vocabulary, and your trip has just been upgraded!

▶ *How to Learn a Language*

◆ Practice on a language app that makes learning a game, like Duolingo or Memrise.

◆ Find "Learn Indonesian" (or whichever language)

channels on YouTube and practice your pronunciation and conversation.

♦ Focus on learning phrases rather than basic vocabulary. For example, instead of learning just the word for "water," learn the phrase "One water, please." Once you understand this sentence structure, you can easily ask for "one coconut, please" or "one ticket, please."

♦ Use flash cards. My college professor taught us that your brain retains 70 percent more information if you write things down. Quiz yourself.

▶ Translation App Dangers

When your four-year-old vocabulary doesn't work, translation apps are a godsend. These days, you can even take photos of foreign text and have them translated in real time. But I do have two pieces of caution when it comes to translation apps:

♦ Translation apps aren't always correct. You may think you're translating a compliment and it translates into an insult. Beware.

♦ If you rely on translation apps too heavily, you will never learn the language. You need to practice speaking and listening.

▶ Still Feeling Totally Lost in Conversation?

Ask the kids for help. When I was living in Bulgaria, I was studying Bulgarian for three hours a day, five days a week. I was learning rapidly, but within three months I had only reached the language proficiency of an eight-year-old. So who became my best friend? An eight-year-old! Her name was Mimi. I could turn to her and ask for a translation of what the adults were saying, and she'd translate for me in words that were in my beginner-level vocabulary.

No Mimis around? Here are three ways to handle language barriers.

- Speak without fear of making mistakes. Let people laugh when you accidentally call the bus stop a blow job (yes, I did this in Bulgaria). It's funny!
- Instead of trying to catch every single word in a sentence, try to catch the overall context of a conversation. Don't stop someone at the first word you don't understand. If you can grab 30 percent of the words, you can usually get the gist of what's happening, and then ask questions later.
- Study nonverbal communication. Emilia loves to hold up her hand and wiggle her pointer finger in a scratching motion when she agrees with something. Like this:

Me: Blackpink is the best K-pop girl group of all time.
Emilia: *(Silently holds up hand and makes a scratching motion with her finger in agreement.)*

It actually took me a year to understand that she wasn't just doing a cute Emy thing and that this finger motion is actually Mexican nonverbal communication that means "Yes, that's right." I didn't figure this out until I went to Mazatlán with her and witnessed her friends do it — then everything clicked, and that was a hilarious conversation.

Learning the hand gestures, the head shakes, and the facial expressions is by far the easiest way to learn to communicate even if you suck at languages.

It's the people who aren't afraid to make mistakes who learn the fastest. Give yourself time and forgiveness, and soon you'll be using words that even your little Mimi doesn't understand!

Quick Quiz

Do you know the top-five most spoken languages in the world?

They are English, Mandarin, Hindi, Spanish, and French — in that order as of 2023.

BOUNDARIES

Last little lesson: You do not have to submit to all cultural norms and customs while traveling.

You're not a jerk. You want to be polite, but being polite does not mean throwing your values and morals aside. As you travel, some cultural differences may leave you offended, annoyed, and outraged.

Some differences require curiosity, while others require boundaries. For example...

A witch doctor putting a curse on you? Not cool. Do not submit.

A sweet Indian auntie putting a red dot on your forehead? Even if you're not married (bindis are often worn by married women), let it happen. Bindis are beautiful, and Auntie is being sweet.

Know your boundaries, and don't be afraid to uphold them. Just because people from one country might be comfortable doing XYZ doesn't mean you have to be. Yes, you are in another culture, and you should do your best to respect that culture and embrace it, but you are allowed to carry your own set of values and bend only when you're comfortable.

Entering a temple in Thailand? I saw a girl on Instagram saying how she felt "body shamed" when she was required to cover her shoulders and knees to enter a temple. Dude, this is a religious custom on religious grounds. Don't want to adhere to religious customs? Then don't enter a temple that requires women to cover their shoulders and knees. Religion is where we draw the line of bending and breaking rules. If it's not aligned with your values, simply don't participate.

Carry your values with you, but don't expect people to change for you. You are the guest. Be respectful. And also, respect yourself.

This may feel contradictory, me telling you to keep your boundaries yet not to push them on other people. But I promise, you'll find the balance in the moment.

One more thing: keep in mind that cultural curiosity goes both ways. Sometimes people will stare at you because you look, walk, and act like an alien compared to everything they know. Have patience because some people may be just as perplexed by your culture as you are by theirs. Remember that while you're experiencing their culture, they are experiencing you!

Congratulations! You're now more equipped than most travelers you will meet struggling with culture shock and boundaries abroad!

CHAPTER 6

Safety and Scary Things

If you ever meet me in person, ask me about the time I spent three days getting a Canadian kid out of jail in Bangkok. Or the time I got such bad food poisoning in Playa del Carmen that I thought I was dying. Or that time I was sitting in the hospital in Chiang Mai holding a yogurt container containing my "sample," which I had brought from home because I was literally shitting blood.

This chapter isn't here to scare you, but it might scare you. And that's great. Because once a story scares you, you don't forget it.

Do not let the things we're about to discuss make you hesitate to travel. Just the opposite. Let the lessons you're learning assure you that you're going to be more prepared than basically everyone who hasn't read this book — and they're still going on their trip, underprepared.

By the end of this chapter, you will have the tools to handle thieves, criminals, bellyaches, and bugs — reducing your chances of falling sick or falling prey.

So are you ready? Are you calm? Okay, good. Now I can tell you about the time I was robbed in Cambodia.

When I was robbed, I was a naive little minnow on my first trip to Southeast Asia, completely oblivious to the dangers hiding in the depths of this destination. I did not research the crime climate beforehand, so I didn't know what to watch out for.

When I landed in Cambodia, I had just finished traveling Thailand, where everything feels welcoming and safe. You feel like nothing can go wrong in the paradise of Thailand. I call this being in "vacation mode," where dangers don't cross your mind. Your guard is down, and your heart is open. (See? I told you you'll feel less afraid once you're traveling!)

This kind of attitude works well in Thailand. In Thailand, you can feel secure carrying your purse around without the risk of it being stolen. Just weeks earlier, I had passed out at a bar on Koh Lanta, and the Rasta bartender covered me with a towel and put my purse in a lockbox behind the counter until I woke up. Not my most responsible moment, but it left me feeling super carefree. A feeling I carried with me into Cambodia.

But this is not what happens in Cambodia. You can't just fall asleep and expect your purse to be there when you wake up. You can't even hang your purse on the back of a chair and expect it to be there when it comes time to pay. Cambodia is one of the poorest countries in Asia, where little kids are trained like ninjas to swipe your stuff. It's actually quite impressive.

But I didn't know that. No one told me that. The blogs I read did not mention the fact that Cambodia requires extra vigilance when it comes to theft. Besides, everyone around me seemed relaxed, and so I relaxed, too.

Cut to the night of the crime: I had just arrived in this little beach town and was ready to party. Most of the bars out there are "cash only," so I made a quick stop at the ATM and took out around $100 USD. In a hurry, I popped back into my teeny hotel room, threw my debit card on the bed (pro tip: don't take your debit card out partying), but forgot to leave some money behind. So now I was on my way to drink myself silly with too much money in my purse.

Okay, I'm going to speed up the story now: After a few beers, my buzz had kicked in, and the Swedish guy sitting in the big papasan chair next to me started looking super fine. I cuddled up next to him, and we started kissing. Then we moved to a bar that was technically closed but only by a tarp, no door. We ducked under the tarp, he threw me on the counter, my purse fell to the sand, and we started reenacting every movie where Blake Lively goes on vacation. Then, right as things were getting steamy, I heard a loud bump and a chair falling over. We were not alone.

Kissing halted, I went to grab my purse and make an escape...except my purse was already gone. A little ninja child had seen us sneak into the bar and was stealth enough to climb under the table in front of us, swipe my purse, and get outta there at lightning speed. For her, it was a game. She was a kid. She was just doing what she'd been trained to do.

So now, not only was I not going to have sex with this Swedish guy in a bar at the beach (probably for the best), but I also came to realize that I had made a huge mistake by leaving all that cash in my purse. And just like that, a week of travel money was gone. (Yes, you can stretch $100 for a week in Cambodia, depending on how modestly you travel.)

Sidenote: I love Cambodia with all my heart. When choosing where to write this book, I chose to go to Cambodia. Don't let this story deter you, let it prepare you.

In hindsight, I don't know if we can really call having my purse stolen during a sexy escapade "a robbery." Instead, we can call this me being a drunk idiot and not taking the proper precautions to protect my belongings.

✈ **TRAVEL LESSON #6** ··

Wear a cross-body purse or fanny pack and do not take it off.

··

When you're out and about, keep your purse on your body even when you're making out with a sexy Swede in a bar. Always keep your cross-body purse or fanny pack on your body, and only carry the cash you need that day. Leave everything else securely in your room, especially if you're going to be drinking.

In addition, please only travel with purses and bags that have zippers. Do not carry a purse or tote bag that has a flimsy snap closure or doesn't close at all. You need a purse or a fanny pack where little hands can't go digging.

I have never made that mistake again because I learned a valuable lesson: thieves and criminals like easy targets. The more experience I have and the more lessons I learn, the harder a target I become. This incident actually happened about eight years ago. Crime hasn't changed much in Cambodia, but I've never had a purse stolen since. Now that I know what to look out for, I know how to prepare and protect myself. Don't be scared — be prepared!

ALEXA'S SAFETY SCHOOL, PART ONE: THE MOST COMMON CRIMES TO PREPARE FOR

1. Opportunistic Theft

The most typical type of theft around the world is the convenient kind. If you leave your phone out on the table and go to the bathroom, it may not be there when you get back.

▶ *How to Stay Vigilant*

Keep your valuables close. Embrace the fanny-pack lifestyle and only carry a cross-body purse with a zipper. Do not have your phone out while walking or riding on a motorbike where someone can easily snatch it from your hands.

If you want to be super safe, get a money belt. They are like fanny packs but super sleek and are relatively undetectable under your clothing.

In especially high-crime areas, double up with both a cross-body purse and a fanny pack or money belt. Keep important stuff (passport, credit cards) in your fanny pack or money belt under your clothes, and keep replaceable items (books, water bottles, sunscreen, towel) in your purse. That way, if someone steals your purse, it won't ruin your whole trip.

Visit my travel store at Alexa-West.com to see the anti-theft and safety accessories I recommend.

▶ *How to Stay Vigilant at the Beach*

What do you do with your stuff when you're on the beach alone and want to go swim in the ocean? If you're in the sand or on a lounge chair, cover your things with your towel so they're harder for a criminal to spot and swipe. Hide your keys under a hat. Wrap your phone in a sarong and bury it in the sand. Just make it hard for a thief to be stealth. Then, go into the ocean, but don't take your eye off your stuff.

To be extra vigilant, find some people who seem trustworthy, ask if they'd mind keeping an eye on your things while you go for a swim, and let them know you're willing to return the favor.

▶ *What Do You Do When Your Valuables Are Stolen?*

Get a police report. Turn that police report in to your travel insurance provider (we'll cover travel insurance in depth in chapter 14) or your credit card company so they can reimburse you via the built-in purchase protection that comes with many travel credit cards (we'll get into this in part 3).

Can't be reimbursed? If you didn't have that item insured or weren't able to get proof it was stolen, that sucks, and you likely won't be getting any money back. Be upset, but also … welcome to the Traveler's Club! You've just earned your first badge — the Stolen Valuables Badge! The more badges you have, the more of a seasoned traveler you are. Do not be discouraged when something "bad" happens to you. Instead, count this as a learning moment and a story to tell. Clean up the mess and keep traveling.

2. Mugging

What do you do if someone tries to grab your purse and run? Hold your bag tight and sit down on the ground. Don't pull back, pull down.

What do you do if someone threatens you with violence in order to get your purse? Give them what they want. Throw your purse in one direction and run in the other.

3. Sexual Assault

We prepare to protect ourselves from spooky strangers, but actually, sexual assault occurs more often between two travelers than between a local and a traveler. Think about it: travelers drink together and often sleep in the same hostels or hotels, so there is more opportunity for things to go awry. But sexual assault is possible with locals as well, especially when being friendly gets misinterpreted as being flirty.

▶ *How to Protect Yourself*

Don't assume a stranger is safe just because he or she is from a culture similar to yours. Bad people come in all packages. Travel is all about trust, so please do trust strangers, but still keep your wits about you. Maintain the ability to listen to your intuition; don't numb it with alcohol. I follow the Three-Drink-Maximum Rule (three drinks per night) when traveling solo.

Rules to follow at night:

- You know the universal rule: do not walk alone at night in iffy areas. If possible, call a rideshare or wave down a taxi even if it's just for three blocks.
- Make sure your doors and windows are locked before bed.
- I walk and sleep with my She's Birdie personal safety alarm. It's an alarm that, when you yank it apart, triggers a siren and flashing light.
- If you're traveling somewhere very iffy, carry a rubber doorstop with you to put on the inside of your door. Let's say a creep tries to enter your room. They will have trouble opening the door, which will give you more time to react. Some doorstops even have alarms!
- Pepper spray is not allowed on planes, but you can look into buying it in pharmacies or online once you land in a country.

So those are the criminal safety things. Now ...

ALEXA'S SAFETY SCHOOL, PART TWO: ILLNESSES, INJURIES, AND DISASTERS

Illnesses

▶ *Stomach Bugs*

They happen. They happen at home, and they happen while traveling. The reality is that you're likely to get sick while traveling because your body is meeting new bacteria and new environments. The good news is that your immune system is getting stronger with every new bacterium and environment it meets.

I've heard of people not wanting to come to Bali because they've heard of "Bali belly" or avoiding Mexico because of "Montezuma's revenge." While I have never had Bali belly in the collective three years that I lived there, I do know people who have. When you have it, it sucks. But it doesn't last forever and should not be a reason to stay home! Here are some ways to avoid and fight tummy bugs everywhere in the world.

- ◆ Before a street food adventure, take two activated charcoal tablets and one Pepto Bismol tablet as a precaution.
- ◆ Don't eat at food stalls that have no customers. This indicates slow turnover of ingredients, which means more time for bacteria to grow.
- ◆ If your tummy starts hurting, consume coconut water, electrolyte drinks, and activated charcoal. Oregano oil is effective in killing norovirus, a common foodborne illness. Turmeric and ginger are fantastic for the healing process once your tummy has settled.
- ◆ If you have diarrhea for more than two days, see a

doctor or pharmacist because you may need prescription medication to kill bacteria or a parasite.

Quick Quiz

True or false?: *You should avoid ice while abroad.*

False! The belief that ice in drinks can make you sick while traveling is a common travel myth. In fact, most ice is made from purified water and is generally safe to consume. On the contrary, I advise you to avoid lettuce and fresh fruits or veggies that have been washed with tap water. (Things that you peel yourself, like bananas and oranges, are safe.) Don't worry about the ice. Instead, confirm that the produce is washed with purified water.

After a stomach bug, the silver lining is that your body will begin to build up the right bacteria to fight off future stomach bugs. The longer you're there, the fewer tummy issues you'll have.

Fun fact: I've only ever gotten food poisoning at Burger King and McDonald's while traveling — including that death's door food poisoning in Playa del Carmen.

▶ Mystery Illness, Bite, or Rash

It may surprise you how accessible medical care is abroad. In many parts of the world you can walk into a pharmacy, ask for the pharmacist's advice, and get antibiotics without a prescription. Or you can walk into a doctor's office and get a prescription quickly, affordably.

When you need medicine from a pharmacist or clinic that

doesn't speak English, here's what to do: go to Google Images and search for the problem you're having + the country you're in. Up will pop pictures of the medication or ointment you need. Show these images to the pharmacist. Or use a translation app. Or just lift your shirt and show them the gnarly rash.

In my travel Facebook groups, girls are always asking questions about rashes or sickness symptoms. A lot of illnesses or irritants are environment dependent, so odds are good that someone in your community has experienced what you're experiencing and can give you advice on which clinic to visit or which cream to purchase.

Also, bug spray. Always carry bug spray if you're in a buggy area.

Injuries

Recently a friend of mine slipped on a stick on a remote island and had to be medevacked to the hospital in Bali. But she was prepared.

♦ She had travel insurance that covered her medevac and care.
♦ She had a short list of trusted hospitals so she could instruct the medical team on where to take her.
♦ She had a travel credit card to cover the hospital bill until insurance reimbursed her.

It is very important, especially in developing countries, that you are taken to a reputable hospital that can give you proper care. If you find yourself in the midst of your emergency, here are two sources to rely on:

Option 1: Your travel insurance. Many travel insurance providers have a 24/7 emergency assistance team who can help arrange medical treatment. Sometimes, they can even coordinate payment directly with the health-care provider, so you don't have to pay out of pocket.

Option 2: A local expat Facebook group. Post about what happened and ask for a firsthand clinic or hospital recommendation. You'll usually get answers within minutes.

If you're not sure whether your injury is serious enough to need a hospital, find a small clinic or pharmacy and see if they can help you. If they can't, they will refer you to a hospital. Just double-check that the hospital they refer you to has a good reputation.

▶ Motorbike Accidents

Motorbikes are dangerous; you know this. But they are especially dangerous when you're driving at night, driving without a helmet, or driving after drinking.

Things to know:

- You don't need a motorbike license to rent a motorbike in most places in the world. However, if you get in an accident, you'll be paying out of pocket for your bike damages and body damages (even more reason to play it super safe when driving).
- Always wear your helmet! If the bike doesn't come with a helmet, rent from another place.
- Always check your brakes. Take your bike on a quick zip around the block to test the brakes before you rent it.
- Take photos of any existing damages to the bike before you leave the shop. This way, they can't claim you made those scratches and charge you more.

◆ If you can avoid riding a motorbike…avoid riding a motorbike.

Disasters

▶ *Natural Disasters*

If you're in trouble, everyone is in trouble. If everyone's in trouble, everyone is working together to solve the problem. You will not be alone.

◆ Have your embassy's number in your phone and know where your embassy is located.
◆ If you're a US citizen, enroll in the Smart Traveler Enrollment Program (STEP); go to STEP.state.gov.
◆ Join the local expat Facebook groups so you can be in the loop on meeting points.
◆ If you're solo when a natural disaster strikes, find the nearest hostel. Hostels are home no matter your age.
◆ Be sure to have travel insurance that includes evacuation coverage for natural disasters.

▶ *Legal Things*

Stay away from illegal drugs! The last thing you need is to be arrested while high. Your "don't do drugs" homework assignment: watch the BBC documentary series *High: Confessions of an Ibiza Drug Mule*.

If you get in trouble, call your embassy. Then call your emergency contact; I recommend having both an emergency contact back home and one locally (so be on the lookout for your next emergency contact friend while traveling). Have these numbers stored in your phone, and write them down on a piece of paper you keep in your wallet. If you ever get caught doing something stupid in another country, remember to ask for a lawyer, and never sign something in a language you don't understand.

All right, so you're not doing drugs, you're not going to be an ignoramus on a motorbike, and you're keeping your purse on your body ... what else shall we worry about?

Ah, yes! Your mother's worst nightmare!

▶ Being Kidnapped and Sold into Sex Slavery

You may have made the mistake of watching the movie *Taken*, where Liam Neeson's daughter gets tricked into sharing a cab with a hot guy at the airport who eventually returns to kidnap her and sell her to evil old men with yachts.

My love, remove this worry from your mind. It is very unlikely that you're going to get kidnapped or trafficked in any of the travel-friendly locations I've mentioned in this book, and here's the totally fucked-up yet true reason why:

If you're reading this book, you are literate, which means you are educated, which means that you have more privilege than most women in the world because you come from a relatively developed country where you likely have rights and where your voice has a decent chance of being heard. Most of the women who are sold into sex slavery, however, have no voice due to their race, culture, or social or financial standing. Kidnappers kidnap people who they hope no one will fight for. This is a very oversimplified explanation of the complexities of human trafficking, but know that most women sold into sex slavery are sold by their boyfriends or family members, rather than randomly snatched while traveling.

If you do notice a creepy man following you, however, here's what to do:

◆ Make eye contact. He needs to know that you see him.
◆ Walk near other women or families. Don't be afraid to approach a nearby stranger, male or female, and tell them you think someone is following you.
◆ Yell, "I see you!" (I've done this before. I had no proof the man was following me, but either way it creeped him out and he kept his distance.)
◆ Pop into a bar and wait a minute, call a cab, or tell the bartender you think someone is following you and ask if someone can walk you home. Seriously, don't be shy to do this.
◆ Have your She's Birdie alarm in your hand.
◆ Consider taking a self-defense class abroad, especially if you're going somewhere that specializes in traditional hand-to-hand combat training, like Thailand (Muay Thai), Japan (karate) or Brazil (Brazilian jiujitsu).

The other stuff you already know: don't walk home by yourself alone at night, don't drink too much, and when possible, use the buddy system if you've met a cool travel friend.

THE TAKEAWAY:
BE CAUTIOUS — NOT PARANOID

We're not going to pretend that dangers don't exist in the world. They do. No country is entirely free of crime. There is no escaping risk. Not at home, not in another country, not on planet Earth — but you can prepare for the curveballs. And you have! You've read this chapter, which means you are now more savvy and less likely to fall victim.

Do not fall into the "be fearless" mindset.

You need your fear! Your fear will tell you when to run

and when to stay. I'm not asking you to be fearless; I'm asking you to be brave. To accept fear and measure it. To move forward knowing that fear will pass. And on the other side of fear is freedom.

The world is full of good people, dreamy places, and safe spaces. There are big brothers, sisters, mothers, neighbors, and fathers all over the world ready to look out for you when you need them. Ask for protection when you need it, and you shall receive it!

Before we wrap this up, let me leave you with some uplifting safety snippets to restore your faith in the world:

◆ In South Korea, you can leave your purse or phone on the table in a bar and usually nothing will happen to it.

◆ Some major destinations, like Mexico City, Dubai, and Japan, have "Women Only" train cars on the subways.

◆ Depending on the country, some rideshare apps have the option to specify "Women Only" drivers.

◆ Most hostels around the world have female-only dorms, and you'll also find female-only hostels (no boys allowed).

And hey, whenever something stressful happens to me, I say, "Universe, you owe me one," and then I wait for the Universe to provide a make-up present, which it always does.

So, my love, you now know what to do to protect yourself, prevent mishaps, and bounce back fast. Just remember: You're not the first girl to travel alone. The world is full of solo female travelers living their best lives as we speak. It's your turn!

Head to my travel store at Alexa-West.com to see a collection of safety gadgets, safe places to travel, and more advice to stay safe while traveling.

CHAPTER 7

Friendship and Loneliness

One evening in Bangkok, I had planned to meet some friends on Khao San Road, but they never showed up (this was before smartphones, when you just had to *find* people). I walked the entire road three times and never found them, but I did spot a table of two girls my age who looked like they were having fun. So I walked up to their table and said, "Hey, I was supposed to meet my friends here, but I can't find them and…" Before I even finished my sentence, they said, "Sit down!" We drank a beer tower. Or two. I can't remember.

Honestly, making friends before smartphones was easy.

Finding them if you lost them, not so easy.

Replacing your lost friends with new friends, easy!

I miss the days when you'd walk into a hostel and everyone was just chatting with each other rather than scrolling on their phones.

I used to live on an island in Cambodia before it had internet, when we still used clicky cellphones with the clicky buttons. No wifi, no data, no smartphones. Time went by slowly. One week in island time felt like one month in real time. This is because we were a lot more present without the internet. You had to fill every hour with *something* or *someone* — or *nothing* or *no one*. You were intentional and carefree all at the same time. So, when you'd meet a stranger, you had no distractions. You were sucked into a vortex of connection without even trying.

When wifi did eventually appear on the island, the hostel where I worked chose to remain wifi-free. So guess which place became the number one spot to hang out? This no-wifi zone, where strangers talked to each other and goofed around like little kids playing in the backyard. We'd come up with dumb games or silly traditions like giving everyone a nickname. And once you have a nickname, you feel like you belong. My nickname was Jellybean.

If someone walked into that hostel and pulled up a seat, there was zero chance that they were scrolling on their phone and a 99 percent chance they were there to be your friend. You'd shout across the bar, "Hey, come join us," and they would. Because they weren't busy on their phone.

There was no guessing. No hesitation to say hi. People just used to talk to each other when they traveled.

I miss those days...but we can still have them.

You know how?

By putting your damn phone away.

You didn't come all the way here just to scroll on Instagram, did you? The next time you're sitting at a bar or on the beach and you have nothing to entertain you, resist the urge to pick up your phone. Resist the addiction. Instead, journal while taking time to look around. Say hello to the person sitting next to you. Read this book. Daydream. Listen to the ocean. Or just sit and watch people walking by.

Hell, next time you need directions, instead of asking Google Maps, do like your ancestors did and ask someone for directions. Give yourself every chance to make human contact, and watch your world spin into beautiful circumstances you never could have planned.

If you show up to a hostel bar, a pool, an airport lounge, or a pedicure spa and you don't bury your face in a phone, the odds that you will make contact or conversation with another traveler or local are extremely high!

No matter how shy or quiet you are, you will not evade social interaction. On the travel trail, friendship will come naturally even if you're the awkward one. You don't need to be charming or funny or good-looking for people to want to talk to you. You just have to show up.

Want to eat dinner alone? Sit with your headphones in, staring at your phone, and no one will approach you.

Want to make friends? Do the opposite. Ears and eyes free so that you are approachable and you notice when someone is trying to get your attention.

I could end this chapter here. It's that simple. But if you're like me, you might have social anxiety, get shy in groups, feel awkward starting conversations with strangers, not typically stay in social hostels, and/or have resting bitch face. In this case, let me help you out.

My social blessing is that I was raised without the internet; therefore, I've got decent social skills. On the other hand, I was given the internet in my twenties, so I know how to use it in ways that enhance my life. Consequently, I am equipped to use both old-fashioned social skills and the World Wide Web to make friends while traveling, like a pro. I'm going to teach you my ways.

Do not chuck your phone in the ocean just yet, but do not plan to rely on your phone to keep you company. Okay? Okay.

The first thing you need to know is this: making friends at home is not the same as making friends while traveling. If a stranger approached you at your local coffee shop at home and asked if they could join you, your Stranger Danger alarm bells would start going off! *Who is this stalker?* But that's not what happens when you're traveling! Travelers are hoping and praying that someone will just talk to them. Be that someone!

HOW TO MAKE THE FIRST MOVE

On another solo evening in Thailand, I went out to a little shack of a restaurant for dinner. I ordered a Penang curry and a Singha beer. At the table next to me was a girl sitting alone drinking a beer, too. No phone. Just sitting and eating and drinking. This made it easy for me to make contact.

> **Me:** Hey, are you drinking alone?
> **Her:** *(Thinking I'm judging her)* Um, ya, I am … why?
> **Me:** Oh, sorry! That's cool. I'm drinking alone, too! Want to drink with me?

And that's how I met Emma from Ireland. We spent the next five nights eating dinner together and were devastated when it finally came time to part ways!

However, Emma's reaction to my awkward opener made it clear that I wasn't so smooth in my approach. So let's talk about how to not be a creep while making friends with other travelers.

Creative Conversation Sparkers

Think back to when you were in kindergarten and would go up to someone and say, "Hey, do you want to be my friend?" That's essentially what's going to happen while traveling but with more on-topic opening lines.

To make contact, you can ask the classic travel questions:

- Where are you from?
- Where are you going?
- How long are you traveling for?

And when you start to get bored of those questions, try these instead:

- What are you eating? Looks good.
- Do you have any food/fun recommendations around here?
- (When someone is just arriving) Where are you coming from?
- (When someone is on their laptop) What are you working on?

If friendship pickup lines aren't your thing, however, here are some strategies that I've found to be very effective.

Eight Friend-Making Strategies

▶ 1. Talk to People You Recognize

As you travel, you'll begin to see familiar faces on the travel path. You'll run into someone on an island that you remember from a previous city, which makes it easy to say ...

Hey, I recognize you from my hostel in Madrid. How's your trip going?

Weren't you on my bus from Barcelona? That was a crazy ride, right?

▶ 2. Ask Other Travelers for Advice, Rather Than Asking the Staff

Instead of only asking reception for recommendations, ask other travelers. People love sharing tips and stories. Just make sure to share tips and stories back! Now you've got a conversation started.

▶ 3. Join Group Activities

I'm obsessed with GetYourGuide.com and Airbnb Experiences. These are two sites that offer group trips and tours that will connect you to other travelers with shared interests.

▶ 4. Invite People to Join You

Don't wait for someone to invite you! Instead, find activities, make plans, create events, and offer invitations!

▶ 5. Carry Your Hobby

Be that person playing the ukulele at a hostel (at reasonable hours). Bring Korean face masks to pass out in your hostel dorm room. Bring your pickleball paddle and go find a court. Show your interests so people have something to grab onto! No hobbies? Bring candy from your culture!

▶ 6. Take a Class or Workshop

Emilia is a painter. When she travels, she looks for painting workshops where she can learn new techniques and spend the afternoon with a room full of people who share her passion. I remember the day she came home from a workshop in Bali elated that she had met the most fascinating woman turned instant friend and creative collaborator.

So, whether it's salsa dancing, basket weaving, or glassblowing, find a class through Facebook groups, noticeboards, or creative centers, and go in with the intention of making a friend while nurturing your talents.

▶ 7. Use Travel Merch

My travel brand, The Solo Girl's Travel Guide (SGTG), uses pink flamingo stickers to identify travel girls that want to make friends with other travel girls! If you put this sticker on your laptop or water bottle and another SGTG girl sees it, she knows that's a sign to approach and say hi! If you have a favorite travel brand and they have similar merch like stickers or T-shirts, bring them traveling! These signals will help you attract your tribe.

▶ 8. Use Food as Bait

Food is a friend maker! I was at a restaurant in Vietnam the other day, and a bored-looking British couple were eating samosas. I yelled over, "Are they good?" and they told me to come try one. I could have politely refused and stayed alone at my table, but I know that food is a friend maker. As I got up to grab a samosa, I read their energy. Sensing that they were open to new friends, I asked, "Can I sit with you?" We sat and drank wine for nearly three hours. Later, the woman told me how glad she was that I had made human contact. They'd been feeling bummed out that everyone had just been staring at their phones rather than trying to make friends.

Don't turn down food, and don't be afraid to offer someone else food. Offering someone food is offering them connection. When someone offers you a stick of gum, you might not want to "take" something away from them, so you refuse. But actually, that stick of gum is a friendship offering. Refuse the gum, refuse the friendship.

Remember that if a traveler wanted to be left alone, they would have stayed home. Or at least they would have stayed in their hotel room.

Make Yourself Easy to Approach

People want to hang out with you, I promise. But approaching strangers is scary unless we're drunk (which is why hostels make so much money from alcohol). Most of us humans carry some degree of social anxiety with us at all times. Even me! I was voted "Most Outgoing" in middle school, but I'm still afraid of rejection and get a little nervous approaching new people. So, when you're too shy (or sober) to approach people, put yourself in situations where you are the approachable one.

▶ *How to Increase Your Chances of Being Approached*

◆ Seek out bars and restaurants with bar seating that makes it easy for someone to sit at a stool next to you.

◆ Replace your headphones with a journal or book or deck of cards.

◆ Illuminate your green light.

What's a green light? It's the invisible light that hovers above your head, indicating to strangers that you're approachable (or not). Instead of an actual light, it's an energy or a vibe. Like a taxicab, you need to illuminate that imaginary green light above your head that says, "I'm available!" And I swear, if you look for it, you can see it lit in other people waiting to be approached.

How to illuminate your green light: Smile, make eye contact, and think over and over in your head, *Green light, green light, green light,* and watch your energy attract new friends.

This Book Has Magic Powers!

Put this book (or any volume of The Solo Girl's Travel Guide) up on your table or somewhere visible. It's a signal to other travelers that you want to make friends. Keep an eye out for fellow travelers doing the same!

Bonus travel fact: Solo travelers are more approachable than groups or couples. If you're solo, you're more likely to be approached.

Okay, so what do you do if you're traveling in desolate areas where it's hard to physically find people? Turn to the internet!

THE BEST WAYS TO FIND FRIENDS ONLINE

During the first three months of a Peace Corps assignment, you live with a host family. After that, you are shipped off to a village where you live alone...and may get kind of lonely. That's what happened to me.

When I lived in the isolated mountains of Belogradchik, Bulgaria, I found it nearly impossible to make friends, so I used Couchsurfing.com to order friends online. I'd advertise my spare room, and travelers would show up on my doorstep like Amazon packages! Both travelers and hosts have reviews, photos, and sometimes background checks. You can choose if you only want to host women or stay with women. You can also approve or deny requests, giving yourself full control — and making this a lot less creepy than it sounds.

So that's Couchsurfing, a platform where people offer their couch or spare room to travelers to sleep for free, whether it be for a night or a few days. Travelers aren't expected to pay for their stay but will usually offer to cook dinner for their host, take them to lunch, or teach them something. Hosts love to show their guests around town or introduce them to their culture, too.

If you're looking for a female-only version of Couchsurfing, join the "Host a Sister" group on Facebook, where women offer a free place to stay, or just friendship, to other women visiting their city.

Try these online friendship-making tools, too:

◆ Join a meetup on Meetup.com, look for Couchsurfing .com meetups, or search for travel girl meetups on Facebook.

◆ Try Bumble BFF. Yes, this dating app has a friend mode!

◆ Find clubs. In Chiang Mai, Thailand, there are writing clubs, book clubs, board game clubs, and pickleball clubs — all of which welcome both travelers and expats. You usually find these clubs on Facebook, via a web search, or by word of mouth.

◆ Join local travel or expat Facebook groups and ask if anyone wants to join you on a day trip or go for a drink. In my travel Facebook group (Facebook.com /groups/sologirlstravelguide) I often see girls asking for a photo friend, aka a partner to visit the sites with and take photos of each other while exploring together.

HOW TRAVEL FRIENDSHIPS WORK

Travel Friendships Move Quickly

When you meet other travelers, you skip the small talk and move straight to the big talk! You tell stories, compare experiences, discuss divorces, and do crazy things so far out of your comfort zone together that the vulnerable side of you can't help but appear.

My best friend and business partner, Emilia, was a Solo Girl's Travel Guide reader first. She bought my Bali guidebook and then messaged me on Instagram. We met for tacos, and within a week, she had moved in with me. Now we have matching tattoos.

Not all travel friendships end in lifelong platonic love, but let me tell you how the best ones usually go:

You set off for Bangkok by yourself. There you meet another traveler who is also looking for travel friends! The two of you spend a day or two exploring together (which, in travel time, feels like a week). She's planning to go north next, but you're planning to go south. When it's time for the two of you to go your separate ways, one of you says, "Hey, I like exploring with you. Come with me and let's travel together for a little while longer!"

And if you've read the room correctly and the other person is also enjoying their time with you, then the two of you enter into a temporary travel buddy relationship. One of you decides to rearrange your plan to carry on with the other's plan, which is cool because now you get to piggyback on someone else's bucket list, making your trip even more spontaneously awesome.

Your adventure has evolved! It has taken on a life of its

own. You are allowing the Universe to guide you toward experiences that you never saw coming! (By the way, this is how I ended up living on an island in Cambodia in 2014. I said yes to canceling my plans to travel with a girl I had just met. If I hadn't, I would not be writing this book right now.)

Travel Friendships Can Sour Quickly, Too!

When you spend so much time with a person, there is a heightened potential for conflict. Be sure to give yourself time and space to be alone — this will reduce your risk of getting sick of each other. Don't be afraid to wriggle free of a travel partner you met along the way. You came alone; you can carry on alone.

WANT TO MAKE FRIENDS WITH LOCALS?

Being a Peace Corps volunteer taught me three important lessons when it comes to making friends with local people:

1. Say yes when a local invites you to dinner — within reason and with common sense, of course.
2. Drink where the locals drink, eat where the locals eat. Even if it's under a tarp outside a minimart. Keep returning to the same local watering holes to build familiarity.
3. Make friends with the people you see every day — the shopkeepers, your neighbors, the street cleaners. Turn the tables and ask them personal questions.

My closest friend in Bulgaria was Cece, the woman behind the counter at an auto-body shop on the corner near my cockroach-infested post-communist block apartment. One day, the cellphone store tried to scam me and told me my bill was

$300 USD. I went into Cece's shop crying. She practically leapt over the counter, pulled me out the front door, and marched me down to that cellphone store by the wrist. She pushed the door open and started screaming as if she was about to rob the place. The "mistake" or "*greshka*" on my bill was quickly fixed. Bless you, Cece.

When I think back on my time in Bulgaria, I think about how much I would have missed out on without Cece. Spending quality time with her, trading stories about life, challenges, triumphs, and daily experiences gave me a greater appreciation and deeper understanding of Bulgarian culture. I practiced my Bulgarian, she practiced her English. She warned me which neighborhoods to avoid. She fed me plenty. And she reminded me that I had someone who always had my back.

LONELINESS

What if you make no friends and are alone for days? First of all, you won't be *alone alone*. You'll have street vendors and hotel staff and the coffee lady. I love being in a little village and saying, "I haven't seen another tourist for days!" This means you're an off-the-beaten-path explorer! You're getting an authentic experience. If anything, travelers are looking for more of this!

But what do you do when you're tooooo lonely?

◆ Call a beloved family member.
◆ Open a homesick letter (essentially a pep-talk letter from someone you love — which we'll talk more about in chapter 18).
◆ Get a massage.
◆ Eat something familiar, like a Snickers bar.
◆ Journal. Write your story.

- Walk around town practicing the language.
- Give city tours and life updates on your social media.
- Build your spiritual practice (we'll talk about this in chapter 9).
- Move hotels or cities or islands to change your environment. It's possible to stay on one street and feel totally alone and then move five blocks over and feel totally seen. Environment is everything.

✈ **TRAVEL LESSON #7** ·····························

Do not wish away your alone time.

···

Alone time is a precious gift. Some people would kill for alone time, and one day you will feel the same way. You'll look back on this trip and feel that you'd give anything just to be in this unbothered, *totally free to do whatever you want* position. So use it! Use this time to get to know yourself. Use this time to explore outside your comfort zone whether that be talking to strangers or meditating in a park. Loneliness is the stage before self-love. Don't give in to loneliness. Use it as a catalyst for discovery and creativity! Remember that your loneliness is not permanent, which is more of a reason to take advantage of it while you have it.

Now I must warn you about something: When you travel, you will find your people. They will become part of your soul, and then you will leave them. For the rest of your life, you will never truly be home in any one place because little pieces of you will be forever scattered around the world. I know you're afraid that you won't make any friends, but baby, your friends are out there waiting for you right this very second. People who will show you that love is real and laughter is medicine. Good things are coming.

Travel Homework

o   Get a head start. Head to Facebook and search for on-line communities in the destination you're headed for. Get a sense of the community before you even leave the couch.

o   Start searching for workshops or group activities you're interested in. Use GetYourGuide, Airbnb, or the search bar in Facebook groups to find activities that interest you.

o   Make a mini–packing list of goodies from home that you want to take to share with new friends during your travels.

CHAPTER 8

Love and Dating

Thank goodness my college boyfriend dumped me. Truth be told, I'm almost sure he dumped me because he was cheating on me. I have no solid proof, but that doesn't matter. What matters is that he's been having sex with that same girl since college. Yep, he married the girl he was probably cheating on me with and had kids with her rather quickly. Meanwhile, I have been dabbling in thrilling romances all around the world throughout my twenties and thirties.

First, there was Svetli. A farm boy that lived in my village in Bulgaria. He spoke no English whatsoever, but he had a car! I'd sneak out my window at night, and we'd go eat omelets in the next village over (*omelet* was the only word I could identify on the Cyrillic menu at the time). He's the reason I learned to speak Bulgarian so quickly.

Pro Tip

The fastest way to learn a language is to date someone who doesn't speak yours!

Next was Ada, a Turkish graphic designer I met at a bar in South Korea. He was an impressive artist but had awful hygiene and chain-smoked. My sheets smelled weird. Now I'm very particular about my man's grooming habits and will never, ever date a smoker.

Then there was Alejandro, a Mexican chef I met in Bali. He was so batshit crazy that my life turned into a full-blown telenovela. I caught him kissing his tortilla maker (a woman, not a machine). I will never date a chef again.

Best of all, there was the guy I met on a bus at 5 AM in Malaysia...

I was headed to the Perhentian Islands to surprise my American friend, Fiona, who was working there as a divemaster. I boarded the minibus bound for bliss with just one seat left. We stopped to make the final pickup, and this super cute guy got on. The driver passed around a clipboard for all of us to write down our information, and as I scribbled my info, I studied his: Oliver, 25, British. The minivan stopped for a food break halfway through the journey, and I decided to do something bold. I walked over to his table and said, "Hi, I'm sitting with you." I sat down, and that was the beginning of an incredible relationship with a total stranger. We didn't get married or anything, but we did fall in love and travel the world together for four incredible years!

Want to know something terrible, though? I never would have swiped right on Oliver back home. He's nearly my height, and based on that alone, I would have filtered him out. I would have robbed myself of the chance to meet one of the world's greatest men. So do yourself a favor while you're traveling and looking for love: ditch the arbitrary rules. Forget "your type." Your type hasn't been working for you anyway.

When you travel, romance can happen when and where

you least expect it — and with a higher likelihood! Think about it: When you're traveling, your daily job is to put yourself out there and meet new people. Even if you're not planning on meeting new people, you're going to be meeting new people! And one of those people could be your person.

With each whirlwind romance, you're exposed to new styles of courtship, communication, affection, and other little love subtleties you've never experienced before. By copy-and-pasting yourself into romantic scenarios with lovers from different countries, you quickly learn what you want and what you really don't want in a partner. More so than if you had just dated people from your own culture (or high school).

In doing this, I was able to reset the standards I held for my love life rather than adopting what I learned by watching Bella Swan commit herself to Edward Cullen for eternity at the age of eighteen. (That's a *Twilight* reference in case you didn't get it.)

If you do fall in love with someone from another country or state, don't overthink it. I get so bummed out when a woman finds a potential match and then says, "I like him, but it will never work. We live too far away." Hello! It's the twenty-first century. With FaceTime, WhatsApp, and freaking airplanes, now is the easiest time in history to make an international relationship work as long as you're open to dating outside the box. Just watch *90 Day Fiancé* if you need further proof.

TRAVEL ACTS AS AN AUTOMATIC DATING FILTER

If you meet a boy or girl, or whatever your preference, on the travel path in Panama or Peru, that means you two already have some major things in common:

✓ You both like to travel.
✓ You're both independent.
✓ You're both hungry for adventure.
✓ You both set goals and see them through.
✓ You're both open-minded to new cultures and customs.
✓ Both of your lifestyles somehow allowed you to take
   time off to prioritize your wanderlust.

Or maybe instead of a fellow traveler, you'll meet a local and end up moving to Italy and having Italian babies. Imagine your baby speaking Italian!

If you're having trouble finding someone you click with at home, pack your stuff and go looking for your person abroad. Here are two real-life examples of beautiful love stories that happened while traveling:

My American divemaster friend, Fiona, fell for another divemaster from Turkey while they were working together in Malaysia. They dated for a few years, got married in Thailand, and are now raising a child together in the US.

My Norwegian friend flew to Thailand on holiday, and even though her mother warned her not to come back with a boyfriend, she did. She fell in love with a Thai guy, and they now own a bohemian beachfront hotel on Koh Chang, where they're raising two adorable Thai-Norwegian children.

I could go on and on with stories like these. When you meet someone on the travel path, don't write them off just because you can't imagine how your love story is going to play out month by month. When you're in love, you begin to realize that the world really isn't that big. These days you can get a job and make money from anywhere, which makes this whole equation totally doable. Just chill. Let it develop naturally! You might have a weekend romance in Amsterdam, forget that person ever existed, and then bump into them three years later and fall in love with them for real. It's all about timing. Plant those little love seeds, and don't worry about how they are going to grow. Just enjoy the planting season — aka the kissing season.

Speaking of kissing, let's talk about Tinder!

ALEXA'S INTERNATIONAL ONLINE DATING SCHOOL

You think Tinder at home is a nightmare? Try Tinder in a foreign country. I know I just fed you a bunch of optimism, but let me be the first to tell you that Tinder abroad can be exhausting. Your location is constantly changing, your languages don't always match up, and your legs are always hairy!

Trust me, you're going to need a quick crash course in online dating abroad before you jump into it. Here we go...

Tinder while Traveling

The first time I downloaded Tinder outside the US was in Vietnam, and my hopes were high! What was I going to find? A debonair diplomat? A French hotelier with a thing for American girls? A philanthropic entrepreneur doing some sexy humanitarian stuff? No. Nope. Not at all. What I found was the lost-and-found bin at the theme park in the sketchy part of town.

As your big sister, I want to make sure you don't waste any time with people who are going to waste yours. As a general example of how travel Tinder goes, here is a list of the men you will find while swiping on Tinder in Vietnam:

- **The guy who messages you and asks you out immediately:** He's asking twenty girls out at once and will absolutely waste your time.
- **The traveler with "Here for a good time, not a long time" in his profile:** He's looking for a one-night stand.
- **The blank profile and one dark photo:** This guy most likely has a girlfriend and is looking to cheat.

But there's always one normal guy or girl for every seventeen undatable ones. If you can scrape your way through the sea of weirdos on Tinder abroad, you can usually find one that's worth your time. We'll talk about what to do when you find a good guy later, but first, let's talk about the garbage men.

I will admit that I have accepted dates with a lot of freaks out of desperation, but I've learned how to streamline them. When you match with another traveler or a local, get to the point of what you're looking for. When they ask, "What are you looking for?" save yourself the energy and calories by being honest.

- **When you simply want someone to show you around:** "I'm looking for someone to explore with."
- **When you're looking for a hookup:** "I'm looking for someone to have a drink with and see where it goes."
- **When you want something serious:** "I'd love to find a person I really click with long-term."
- **When you're open to all possibilities:** "I'm open to all possibilities."

Or don't wait for them to ask. Just tell them what you need 'cause you don't have a lot of time before you move on to the next destination. Being coy and casual will only eat into your precious travel time.

Yes, finding love and getting laid would be nice and are possible, but plan to use Tinder to find an exploring buddy rather than the love of your life. Then, when the pressure is off and you're not even thinking of love, you just might fall in love. That's how it always works.

Want to Start Dating Abroad Now?

Try Tinder Passport or Bumble Travel Mode. This is where you can set your location to anywhere! If you're in the US and about to fly to Singapore, you can start swiping in Singapore and arrange a couple dates ahead of time.

Rules for Meeting an Online Date in Person

Since you're swiping all the way on the other side of the world, where you don't know the streets, your best friend can't come rescue you, and you likely don't speak the local language, you need to take extra precaution. The same dating safety rules from home apply out here, and I'd like to add a few more:

- Don't go on a date unless you have data on your phone in case you need to make a quick escape.
- Have rideshare apps downloaded on your phone before you go on your date. Even better, have your credit card connected to the app so you don't have to worry about whether you have money for the ride.
- No rideshare apps available? Have local taxi numbers in your phone or at least be familiar with how you're going to get yourself home. Know when subways stop working or buses stop running.

- Have your hotel location and phone number saved in your phone.

- Screenshot his or her profile and send it to your bestie at home or in town. Just make sure *someone* knows who you're with.

- Share your live location with your bestie.

- Let your date know that you have done both of the above, which may deter him from doing anything sketchy.

- If you feel comfortable, let your date walk you to the door of your hotel or into the lobby.

- Carry your She's Birdie alarm.

- Date at solo girl–approved date spots. With the help of women around the world, I've compiled a list of date spots that are approved for solo girls. These places are in safe locations, and some spots are so official that the staff are expecting my girls (you) to start bringing their dates here, so they'll keep an extra eye on you. You can see and add to a list of female-approved date spots around the world at Alexa-West.com/OneWay.

WHERE AND HOW TO FIND ROMANCE WITHOUT THE INTERNET

If meeting someone online isn't your thing, you'll be pleased to know that it's easy to make romantic connections in real life while traveling. Yes, in real life! That still happens!

Here are places where I have organically met love interests while traveling:

On a bus
At a hostel

At a hotel bar
On a food tour
In an airport lounge
While volunteering
During an Airbnb Experience
With my scuba instructor (but that was a mistake)

Wow, that's a lot of guys. Go, me! But honestly, meeting them was easy. Natural even, because the travel trail is designed to facilitate social interaction. I just had to show up and illuminate my green light. Yes, the green light works on romantic partners, too, because the best connections start with a friendship.

Now, let's say you met someone you really like, but both of you are traveling. How do you turn a travel kiss into a travel relationship?

Approach #1: You could let it happen naturally. If it's meant to be, it's meant to be.

Approach #2: You could understand that your window of being in the same place at the same time is short, so you need to be feisty. This isn't the time to be shy or play it cool. If you like someone, ask them out. If you want to see someone again, tell them. If you want someone to cancel their plans and come with you to the next island, be bold and invite them!

Don't be afraid to make big moves. What's the worst that could happen? You never see them again?

HOW TRAVEL RELATIONSHIPS WORK

Okay, so, congratulations! Your love interest decides to join you! Now let me be the first to tell you that travel relationships escalate quickly — but it never feels "too fast." Out here, you are free to fall head over heels for someone and spend every night and day getting to know them. There are no rules or schedules to follow. No judgment. No pressure. You just do what feels right.

Plus, it's easier to chase romance while traveling because you don't have the same obligations to manage as you do back home. Back home, you likely have a full-time job or at least a routine! Back home, when you start dating a new person, you only see them a couple nights a week, depending on your schedule and theirs. Love typically moves more slowly back home — but not out here!

Out here, you find someone you click with, your travel plans melt together, and you skip ahead to the intimate stuff.

"Intimate stuff" includes the not-so-glamorous stuff, too. You're going to floss, snore, take off your makeup, get hangry, smell sweaty, talk about money, and expose your most vulnerable cards almost immediately. The cool thing about this is that you swiftly find out whether or not you mesh.

But just because you like someone doesn't mean that they won't drive you crazy …

Travel Love Dangers to Expect

A traditional relationship at home gives you and your partner space for eight hours a day. Then you have mini-reunions at night where you (in theory) enjoy catching up with each other within a familiar routine. But a travel relationship is not like that.

Let's say you find your person and decide to travel the world with them. That means you're about to spend 24/7 in their presence, and there is no avoiding their irritating little habits. On top of that, cultural challenges can bring out the worst in you. There's no hiding who you genuinely are on a grueling travel day. The person you're dating is going to see the real you, and you're going to see the real them — almost immediately.

This constant proximity while in a pressure cooker of cultural challenges brings every issue/revelation/observation to the surface. When things go wrong, tension builds, and romance can dissolve if you're not on guard.

The number one killer of travel relationships = not enough space. Here's how to avoid that.

✈ **TRAVEL LESSON #8** ·································

An hour a day keeps the breakups away.

···

Get away from each other for at least an hour a day. Go on a walk, read on the beach, work at a café, take a dance class — anything to give yourself a little distance, even if you don't think you need it. Give yourselves a chance to miss each other. And for the love of God, never, ever become an Instagram couple. It's so much pressure.

BIRTH CONTROL WHILE TRAVELING

You're having sex all over the world, and I couldn't be happier for you! But as your big sister, I want to talk about birth control. If you're not on birth control before you start traveling, I recommend that you start making a birth control plan now.

Get your birth control at home, or see if you'll be able to access birth control in your destination country. I am a huge fan of medical tourism, or going to another country that offers high-quality medical or dental care at more affordable prices than home. For example, I got my IUD in a fancy hospital in Bangkok where they treated me like a queen, sending a car to pick me up for my appointment and assigning me a medical concierge to take me through the entire experience. She even held my hand during the procedure! My IUD cost $300 in Thailand without insurance, whereas my previous IUD cost $900 in the US *with* insurance.

To find a good gynecologist abroad, I ask for recommendations in female Facebook groups, whether they're country-specific like "Girls in Bali" or more general like "Girls Who Travel." To save time, use the search bar in the group and search for "birth control," or make a post and you'll get first-hand recommendations and possibly prices, too.

You can also get the shot, the implant, pills, and the morning-after pill in many countries over the counter without a prescription. In fact, one hundred countries throughout the world offer birth control over the counter. As in, you can just walk in and ask for it without a prescription. Search for your destination + "birth control" and see what you can access.

And carry condoms. Even if you're on birth control, always use condoms while traveling! An STI is not a souvenir that you want to bring home.

LAST NOTE: THE BEST PLACE FOR A BREAKUP

...is on the other side of the world where you can't show up at your ex's doorstep and beg them to change their mind. Or string each other along for months when you could be moving on. Pack your shit and get on a plane. Go cry into the pool. Get drunk under the sun. Yell at the moon. Sob to perfect strangers who end up holding your hand and crying with you. Let the heartbreak out into the world and move on with a tan.

Dream Partner Visualization

Hey, single women and breakup trippers (or women who wish they were single and are thinking about a breakup trip): What do you want in your next relationship?

Make a list of everything you want in your ideal partner. Make it exhaustive, five pages long if it needs to be, and sleep with it under your pillow. Read it often. Refrain from telling yourself that this is a creepy thing to do. It's not. I did this for five months and met a man who exactly matched my list. I got everything I asked for … but I also didn't get what I didn't ask for. Be specific about what you need 'cause this stuff works.

PS. I cannot resist getting involved in your love life! I've created a free printable Dream Partner Visualization template so that you can get super clear on what it is you want in a partner. Get it at Alexa-West.com/OneWay. And if you do meet the love of your life as a direct result of this magic manifestation, then please invite me to the wedding.

CHAPTER 9

Hard Days and Happy Days

My healer in Bali taught me...

✈ **TRAVEL LESSON #9** ·······································

In every "bad" situation, look for the gift.

··

The best way to explain this to you is through a story that everyone told me not to tell you, but I can't help myself.

It was 5 AM in my beachfront bungalow in Cambodia when I was awakened by a rustling sound coming from under my pillow. Thinking it was a mouse, I sat up quickly to remove the pillow and the mouse... but the noise came with me. The rustling wasn't coming from under the pillow — it was coming from inside my ear!

A bug had crawled inside my ear cavity and was scratching around on my eardrum! I catapulted out of bed, threw on my bathing suit, and sprinted into the ocean, submerging my ear underwater trying to kill whatever had crawled inside the hole in my head.

And then I saw gift number one: I looked up and noticed

that my bug friend had woken me up to watch the most beautiful sunrise I've ever seen. I took in the moment while floating in warm ocean water on a gorgeous island. I had a creature living in a hole in my head, but my gratitude couldn't be shaken. This is what happens when you practice gratitude on a daily basis: eventually it becomes ever-present and a travel superpower.

When drowning the bug didn't work, I sought help.

Gift number two: Lying on a wooden floor under a thatched roof as the hotel manager poured warm olive oil into my ear for an hour and a half while I sipped a beer through a straw and listened to her inspiring life story. While I lay there as her captive audience, she told me how she had left her husband, sold her house, and quit her job and had been living on this island in total delight for three years. After that, the bug died (RIP Henry) and I was left with so many gifts! I saw a gorgeous sunrise, made a dear friend who helped provide inspiration for this book, and now I know what to do if anyone else should wake up at 5 AM with a critter in their ear (drown it with warm oil, and it will dissolve or dislodge).

Although I should have been panicking, I was only mildly distressed. I remained grateful that I wasn't in pain and decided to find the humor in the fact that I was walking up to random people and asking them if they had any experience in getting a bug out of an ear. I was exceptionally social that day.

So I'm not going to lie to you and tell you that traveling is comfy and cozy and cute all the time. It's not. But baby, you don't want comfy and cozy and cute all the time. You want surprising, challenging, and unexpected! You want to be a wild explorer, not a comfort zone tourist. You want crazy stories to tell your grandkids. Or stories to tell somebody else's grandkids if you decide not to have kids — which is totally acceptable.

On Bug Day, I stayed positive! But the next day, I found myself feeling completely drained. Partly because of the bug fiasco and partly because I was entering week three of traveling. By week three, you will experience mental fatigue. The planning, the moving, the translating — it can be a lot of work. So please know...

TRAVEL BURNOUT IS A THING

A day will come when you need a vacation from your vacation. When you wake up and just feel overwhelmed. Your travel brain has run out of juice, and you need a Nothing Day to recharge. Just like back home, we need self-care days.

When you start feeling burned-out, give yourself permission to have a Nothing Day with no guilt and no shame. Stay in bed and exist without ambition. Don't put pressure on yourself to snorkel or hike or do anything heroic. My Nothing Days usually involve reality TV, getting a massage, and having pizza for dinner. No thinking required.

Rule #1 for Nothing Days:
Don't Stay in Your Room All Day

Even though you're releasing yourself from all responsibilities, staying in bed and isolating yourself will actually make you feel worse. Once you're feeling even a little bit low, it's easy to spiral into pseudo-homesickness. Eventually, you'll need to get out of bed, go for a walk, and get something to eat. Coax yourself out of your hole with things that bring you joy.

Rule #2 for Nothing Days: Expect Plot Twists

A funny thing happens when you wipe your schedule clean: There tend to be unexpected developments to your day!

When you let go of control, life loves to surprise you. Like that one time I went to get a snack from a minimart in Thailand with plans to take it back to bed and watch *Married at First Sight* under the covers…but wound up taking ecstasy on a mountain in my pajamas with a group of Canadians who convinced me to get in their truck outside said minimart. When you expect nothing, you usually end up getting something extraordinary.

THREE WAYS TO HAVE HAPPY DAYS

1. Become a Mood-Watcher

Emilia taught me, "Treat yourself like you'd treat your best friend." This is especially helpful because my best friend Emilia herself is a feisty Latina who breathes fire whenever a man touches me or someone disrespects me. That girl has my back 'til death do us part. While Emilia is one of the kindest souls I've ever met, she's also human. I have come to know her triggers and her moods, so I am always ready to give her a pep talk, physically restrain her, or do her eyeliner on a day she's feeling frumpy.

This little mantra from Emilia has changed the way I travel. I now practice self-care and self-love wherever I go. I have become a mood-watcher of myself: *Oh, she's getting cranky? Her blood sugar is low. I've got an emergency granola bar in my purse! Oh no, is she about to rage at the kid playing* Call of Duty *without headphones? Pop in those noise-canceling earbuds and let her listen to Corey Taylor acoustic.* Know what you need.

This self-monitoring trick has the power to change your whole trip (and your whole life) from stressful to stressless. This lesson expands beyond travel. No matter where you are and what stage of life you're in, becoming your own best friend is the most empowering thing in the world. It means acknowledging your strengths and weaknesses, embracing your quirks and flaws, and loving yourself unconditionally without giving a damn what anyone else thinks. To be all you need on the good days and the sad days. To comfort yourself and give yourself grace without judgment. To give yourself whatever you need to write the story you've always wanted to live. That is a gift that solo travel gives you.

2. Keep a Morning Routine

Give yourself something to control. Check in with yourself every morning. Keep at least one thing consistent and holy, and that is your morning routine. Wake up with gratitude, set an intention for the day, drink a big glass of water, do some EFT tapping (more on this soon), and move your body! This is my exact mini-routine that I carry with me all over the world.

Most often, I'll do a Chloe Ting workout in my bungalow (when I have the space), or I'll throw a towel on the floor and do some gentle stretching for ten minutes. Some days, I might go for a walk on the beach while listening to an audiobook or take a yoga class. The goal is to connect my brain with my body in order to feel aligned. Plus, endorphins.

If you're thinking, "Screw you, Lexi. I didn't come on vacation to work out," that's fair. But I'm telling you, ten minutes of stretching just to get in touch with your body will set the tone for how you feel all day long, no matter what you wear or what you do. This is not about what you look like, by the way. It's about how you feel. When you feel powerful in your body, you feel powerful in your mind.

Speaking of bodies…

3. Embrace Juicy Bodies, Grandmothers, and Bathing Suits

I am not a petite size 4. I have thick thighs and a tummy and a really uncommon 38B bra size. When I was living in South Korea, I was quickly taught that I do not belong in boutique clothing stores. I didn't learn this by trying on clothing. I was never given the chance. Shopkeepers would see me coming and stop me at the door. They'd use both of their arms to make a big X and say, "No size." Translation: "Hey American girl, you're too big for this store."

The first time this happened to me, I was insulted. The second time, I was enraged. The third time, the shopkeeper squeezed my breast when she told me, "No size," and I was slightly flattered that it was my luscious rack that made me a noncandidate for her baby clothes.

Point is, if you do not look like a model or a South Korean college student, shopping or just existing in countries where women are petite or not the same size as you can be triggering. And if you're headed to a beach destination where you're going to live in your bathing suit, this can be downright terrifying.

Not to mention, mothers and grandmothers on every continent love to comment on your weight daily. Today you're fat. Tomorrow you're skinny. Sometimes it's flattering, and sometimes it means that no one will marry you.

So, from one non–Victoria's Secret model to another, let me tell you how I survive and thrive while traveling in my skin.

▶ My Body-Confidence Superpower

Anytime someone makes you feel like you're not beautiful enough or small enough or curvy enough, use this technique:

Think of all the women who look like you. Think of women your size. Would you ever want them to feel ashamed of their bodies? Would you ever want them to think that their ankles aren't perfect, their back fat is ugly, or their nose is wrong? No! Never!

Now imagine a girl with a similar body type sitting across from you, having a moment of self-doubt or being bullied about her looks — how would you react? What pep talk would you give her? How would you protect her? Would you punch someone in the face for her? Now take that protective energy and put it on yourself.

Choose to love the way you look on behalf of yourself, but also on behalf of every woman who looks just like you. Pretend that you are the unapologetic ambassador of your body type, and spread empowerment by embracing your body with confidence no matter how many damn Instagram models you're surrounded by. There's more of us than them, by the way. Jiggly belly girls, unite!

So, even though I'm not a size 4, I'm wearing my goddamn bikinis, and I hope that every girl who sees my perfectly imperfect body gets the message that we are beautiful just the way we are. I hope my choice to love myself reminds other girls who look like me to do the same.

One more thing. Don't take your body for granted. It does amazing things for you, including taking you on this trip. If your left leg was gone tomorrow, you'd think, *I wish I'd appreciated my leg instead of criticizing it.* So make a promise to yourself to find balance in your body while traveling. Stretch in the morning, and then give yourself permission to just eat the damn churros in your swimsuit. Life is too short.

You will encounter all sorts of beauty standards and ideals around the world regarding weight, skin color, eyelids, nose bridges, and butts. While I love beauty tourism and playing within the world of beauty, I also like to remember that I don't have to conform. I can be my own brand of exotic everywhere I go.

A Sad Beauty Encounter with a Stranger

"No, not beautiful. Not white," said the gorgeous Vietnamese woman selling carrots in the market after I showed her a photo I took of her. In Asia, dark skin is associated with lower-class farmers, and whiter skin is associated with privilege. So much so that skin-whitening products are sold and advertised everywhere. Westerners want to be tan because it signals that we went on vacation or have the time to spend outdoors, while other people may want to be white because it signals they have money, work inside, or don't work at all. Funny how the world works.

GROW YOUR SPIRITUAL PRACTICE

If you want to travel and not lose your mind, you need a spiritual practice. If you want to travel and discover your purpose, you need a spiritual practice.

When I moved to Indonesia, I was a full-on atheist. I rolled my eyes at everyone who used words like *manifest* or *the Universe*. And then, Bali happened.

One night I went to some woo-woo lady's house for something called a "past-life regression." In the backyard there were yoga mats arranged in a circle with a glowing fire in the middle. Standing near the fire was a woke dude wearing lots of bracelets and holding both a drum and a large feather. I didn't know what was supposed to happen, so I was like, *I'm just going to take a nap while all these hippies pretend to talk to God.*

The ceremony began and, as if the Universe turned on a vacuum, I was sucked into another world. Suddenly, I was standing with my grandparents in a field near the house I grew up in. My grandmother opened up a jewelry box, and inside was my soul mate. Not like a tiny man, but the essence of him. She pointed across the field to an opening in the forest and said, "He's waiting for you over there." I began to walk, and then I ran. Our eyes met, and I jumped into his arms. Five months later, I met this man in real life on a dating app.

A few years ago I would have said, "You're all faking it," but after a couple months in Bali, the existence of God or the Universe or whatever you want to call it is undeniable. With each encounter like this, I stopped being so stubborn, my spiritual practices were created, and my life changed.

Alexa's Spiritual Tool Kit

I still don't subscribe to any religion, but I talk to the Universe and my higher self every day. Calling on your intuition to guide you rather than leaning on your logic is sometimes the most logical thing to do. Whenever you feel alone or lost, a spiritual practice will guide you back to your true north. Here are my go-to practices:

◆ **Visualization exercises:** Silent meditation does not work for my busy brain, but lying down, closing my eyes, and allowing myself to be guided into a recorded meditation or a visualization has sincerely changed my life. Start by searching for "Guided Visualization Meditation — Lisa Nichols" on YouTube.

◆ **EFT tapping:** EFT stands for emotional freedom technique. You tap on meridian points on your body (kind of like acupuncture without needles) while speaking mantras that calm you or inspire you. It feels silly, but it's rooted in science. Try it with Gala Darling on YouTube. She's the galactic goddess of EFT tapping, and she's changed my life.

◆ **Mirror work:** Author and motivational speaker Lisa Nichols talks about this, too: the power of staring in the mirror every morning while repeating positive mantras. Again, YouTube it. There are experts out there who can guide you through mirror work not just on bad days that you want to turn around, but also on an intentional journey to level up in life. The way we talk to ourselves creates our reality. Start in the mirror.

◆ **Calling on your higher self:** Your higher self is you at your spiritual core, beyond your body and this human experience. Your higher self embodies intuition. When I'm facing a problem, I call on my higher self to sit next to me or across from me and I ask her for advice. I duplicate myself and visualize that the hottest, most confident, and calmest version of myself is sitting next to me. I turn to her to lead me toward the choices or answers that align with the best solution or outcome possible. When you take away the bullshit, drama, and overthinking, you discover that your intuition and higher self always know what to do.

◆ **Oracle cards:** For an advanced spiritual practice, I recommend buying one of Rebecca Campbell's oracle decks and learning how to use these decks to connect to your higher self.

✈ **TRAVEL LESSON #9.5** ··································

Being positive is a strategic choice.

···

Travel is life amplified. The good stuff feels really good, and the tough stuff feels really tough. So I want to end this chapter with a very important perspective-flipping lesson: When you get a bug in your ear or a grandma calls you fat, flip your negative emotion into a positive one by saying, "I'm glad this happened because…" and finish the sentence with a gift. There's always a gift if you choose to see it. Make it a game and watch how quickly you can turn a bad travel day into a wonderfully memorable one. If you can practice this one mantra for your entire trip, I guarantee you, it will spill over into your entire life.

CHAPTER 10

Finding Your Purpose

Sorry to ruin the fantasy, but sitting on a beach in Puerto Vallarta isn't going to solve your problems. In fact, your problems will sit right there next to you looking out into the ocean, living their best problematic life! You can't run from your problems because your problems can run, too! Sometimes, in fact, your problems will feel even more profound on an empty island or in a foreign city where you're forced to face them without your usual coping mechanisms or support circle.

Things that you never knew bothered you suddenly bother you. These could be new problems or problems you brought from home. A familiar smell or a seemingly unrelated activity can cause buried memories to resurface when you least expect them. While you're zip-lining through the jungle, you may suddenly have a flashback to that time your hamster died and your brother blamed you. You spiral into being really mad at your brother during the entire trip, wondering why your childhood was so unfair, feeling the need to return home and buy a new hamster to repair the childhood wound that zip-lining had suddenly, inexplicably released. Or your problem might be simpler, like the torture of chub rub (when your thighs chafe with every step), which can negatively affect your day.

Call these annoyances, stressors, pains in the ass — whatever — but for efficiency's sake, we'll just call them problems.

Some problems are meant to be counseled, some are meant to be drowned in the ocean, and some are meant for something special. Here's a truth that no one teaches us growing up, a true *aha* revelation that can change your life if you let it. Are you ready?

✈ **TRAVEL LESSON #10** ·····································

Your problems are your purpose.

···

Let me say it again. Your problems are your purpose.

Ask someone, "What's your purpose in life?" and they'll say, "Heck if I know," but ask someone, "What are your problems in life?" and they'll give you a list.

Think about some of the most successful companies from the inside out. They all started to solve a problem.

Problems with dating created dating apps.

Problems with feeling floppy created Spanx.

And problems with traveling solo as a woman created my company. I ugly-cried my way backpacking through Southeast Asia, wishing I had a big sister who would have warned me about all the bullshit I continued to encounter as a female traveler. But that big sister didn't exist, so I became her. I solved my own problem, and in turn, I solved the problems of thousands of girls who were experiencing the same problem as me.

Get how this works?

When you find a problem that doesn't have a solution, you may be the solution. While you're traveling, pick a problem (or let that problem pick you) and fall in love with it. Become obsessed with solving it, and voilà, you've found your purpose. Or at least, *a* purpose, because you can have more than one. Let your bummers be your blessings, I say!

WHAT DOES A PURPOSEFUL PROBLEM LOOK LIKE?

Not every problem is negative. Some problems are fun, so in this case, we call them puzzles. The puzzle of global connection created the internet, and the puzzle of eating pizza on the go created Hot Pockets (I love Hot Pockets).

Am I suggesting that your purpose in life might be to create a product to rub on your thighs so they don't chafe when you walk? Yes, I certainly am! If you created an anti–chub rub solution, a stick that glides on a woman's thighs and doesn't rub off in tropical climates, you'd be solving a problem for millions of women (and even men) with juicy thighs. This seemingly silly little idea serves a purpose. The purpose is to make women more comfortable. Now that they're more comfortable, they can be more present. They can focus more on exploring, rather than the pain between their thighs! They feel more confident and less like a marshmallow on fire. They're happier, and that happiness spreads.

You, as the chub-rub stick creator, facilitated that (and maybe made a ton of money in the process).

Are chub-rub sticks or Hot Pockets going to change the world? They just might. If we were all creating things that made us happy in order to make others happy, the world would be a happier place. Don't you agree?

Whatever little idea is in your head — to solve a problem or a puzzle — it's been planted there by the Universe to be born through you. Either you take that idea and bring it into this world or that idea floats on to find another mother to give it life.

Have you ever had a genius idea, done nothing with it, and then five months later seen that exact idea pop up on a billboard or in a store? That idea was determined to be born. You didn't birth it, so the idea found someone else who would give it life. Read the book *Big Magic* by Elizabeth Gilbert. She explains this concept much more poetically than I ever could, but the gist is that your idea isn't stupid, it's supernatural. It's magic waiting to be made manifest.

TRAVEL TO YOUR PURPOSE

I bet you thought I was going to tell you that your purpose had to be something extreme like giving up all your earthly belongings and moving to a yurt in Mongolia to dedicate your life to humanitarian work, right?

No. Purpose looks different for everyone. For some people, their purpose is indeed humanitarian — but for others it's being a mom who raises incredible humans or a landscaper who makes neighborhoods more beautiful. Maybe it's being a lash technician who makes women feel prettier. Maybe it's being a nurse. A librarian. A food reviewer. A school bus driver. A counselor. A bird-watcher. A dog walker. A flight attendant.

Or perhaps your purpose is having a problem with someone else's problem. Maybe your purpose lies in exposé documentary filmmaking or politics.

Or perhaps you already know your purpose. Maybe you're already living it as a kick-ass teacher or a talented quilt maker. In that case, can you turn that magic up a bit? Can you chase your purpose harder? Can you travel with it, see it from a new perspective, and take it to the next level?

That's what travel does. There is a reason the "travel to find yourself" cliché exists. Many clichés are rooted in truth. Finding yourself or discovering your purpose is easy when you're traveling. Away from the interruptions of home, travel gives you the time, space, and perspective to look at the world and see your role within it more clearly. Travel acts as a transcendental lens to change your perspective on where you are in life, no matter what you're doing — purpose or no purpose.

When you travel solo, you have ample time to sit alone, wander alone, and ponder alone. This is why I tell you not to wish away your alone time. Use it as holy time to reflect on who you are, what you've been through in life, and more importantly, what you desire next.

One last *maybe* of the day: maybe your purpose is to simply focus on being the best version of yourself, resolving your pain and healing your trauma so that you can spread more joy and support to the people you love. Your support may be a catalyst to change the world.

You may think your little idea is too little, but if you can love it enough, you can grow it so big that it sends ripples to everyone you come in contact with — whether that's strangers on a bus or the millions of people who come to hear you speak on stage.

So traveling isn't going to fix all your problems, but it will force you to face them, and if you face them with the right mindset — that is how your magic thing can be born. Your magic, your purpose, your mission.

Your purpose doesn't have to be your moneymaker. This purpose might not make you a billion dollars, but it will shift the way you feel about your life. Possibly overnight. You might stay in the job you have and pursue your purpose out-side of work — which in turn will make you happier, which will snowball into you being more motivated to wake up in the morning, which will spiral into you doing better at your job and getting a promotion or finding more success in your interpersonal relationships — which is the secret to being a fulfilled human on Earth.

Or your purpose might just make you a billion dollars! You never know!

Whether at work or after work, your purpose needs to exist somewhere in your life. Otherwise, what's the point in living?

Let me tell you a universal secret: What you're seeking is seeking you. What you want wants you more. What's meant for you will not pass you by. You just have to listen to hear your calling — then answer it.

VISUALIZE IT

Still having trouble finding your purpose? Believe me when I say, if you can visualize it, you can actualize it. Think about the fact that everything is created twice. Songs, art, businesses, airplanes — all of it. These were first created in someone's imagination. Second, in reality. Dream it first.

Visualization is key. Visualization practices are how I've manifested every dream into reality, including this book. So daydream in the shower, on the bus, in bed at night. Create your wildest fantasies, and when you're ready to work on your purpose, meet me at Alexa-West.com/OneWay, where I will lead you to some powerful visualization exercises to take your dreams to the next level.

Thought Break

What do you daydream about in the shower? What do you fantasize about when you're stuck in traffic? These dreams have come to you for a reason. Don't ignore them. Play with them, become obsessed with them, and write them down. They'll take you somewhere.

PART THREE

YOUR EXIT STRATEGY

CHAPTER 11

How to Afford This When You Think You Can't Afford This

The idea of packing everything up to travel the world is romantic, but is it financially possible? Travel is for rich people, right?

No.

Please believe me when I say that travel makes making money and saving money easier. I'll say it again: travel makes making money and saving money easier — not harder! If done correctly, travel is the secret to getting out of debt and escaping a life of struggle. Contrary to what your old-school dad might believe, traveling can be a financially responsible move. Travel can significantly lower your monthly expenses (rent, transportation, entertainment) depending on the destinations you choose to live in or roam around.

This is why I've lived predominantly in Southeast Asia for ten years, throughout my twenties and early thirties. A decent apartment with a pool in a central, safe location in Thailand can cost around $400 per month depending on the area. And as a woman on a mission to discover herself without having to sell her soul to a 9-to-5, that path in life has always been more appealing than struggling to pay rent and feed myself in Seattle.

How much does your rent (or mortgage) cost at home?

According to the US Bureau of Labor Statistics in 2020, Americans spent an average of around 35 percent of their income on housing. For young people starting out in low-paying jobs in urban areas, it's often much more. In other words, over a week out of every month, you're working just to pay rent. The other 65 percent of your income is spent on utilities, groceries, eating out, entertainment, car payments, and transportation — mostly. You're in the lucky minority if you can put what's left over toward a savings account.

So, when you travel, if you're traveling to affordable locations and choosing accommodations wisely, your cost of living can significantly decrease, and the way you spend and save can significantly improve.

Have loans? Move to South Korea and teach English for a year. One of my fellow teachers, Lauren, was able to pay off $10,000 in student loans in one year while living in a new country, experiencing a new culture.

Building a business from scratch? Start house-sitting or pet-sitting to cover your living expenses while traveling. With your accommodations paid for, you have all the time in the world to focus on establishing your business.

Traveling on a budget? Volunteer at a hostel or find a gig on Workaway.com so that your food and housing costs are covered, allowing you to spend slower and travel longer. While you're at it, pick up some freelance gigs online to sprinkle some more cash flow into the equation.

Working remotely? Move somewhere with a cost of living that stretches your salary. You can cut your monthly expenses in half while saving *and* treating yourself to massages, beautiful places to stay, and eating out often just by choosing your location strategically.

Just want to be able to afford an enjoyable existence on Earth? Relocate to a city where you don't need a car to get around, where you're not expected to tip 20 percent on every damn thing you buy, and where a medical bill won't bankrupt you.

All this is a totally accessible reality that, for some reason, many still consider a "risky" move. I'm here to prove just the opposite. Without travel, I would still be struggling to make ends meet. Instead of settling for struggle, I chose a different route. Instead of working a job I would resent to pay for an apartment I could barely afford, I moved abroad, lowered my cost of living, and saved money. I used that money to start a business, and now I make enough money to live wherever I want. And I made it this far without any credit card debt. In fact, I have excellent credit!

Travel was absolutely my ticket to financial freedom.

Mastering this *work + travel* equation isn't a fluke that only worked for me. It worked for my best friend, Emilia, who started her own graphic design agency that lets her consult with her clients from anywhere in the world. It worked for my friend Laura, who teaches English at a fancy international school in Bangkok with a fantastic salary. It worked for Christian LeBlanc, a guy who created an empire by traveling with his camera. It worked for my brothers. I could go on and on and on. Travel can be a smart money move when done correctly!

HOW MUCH MONEY DO YOU NEED TO TRAVEL?

The possibly irresponsible but sometimes true answer is: Whatever's in your pocket.

As I've said, I left the US with just $200, and while I don't recommend that, it can work. I had a job lined up with the Peace Corps, so I knew that my cost of living was covered. Same thing when I moved to South Korea: I left with $800, knowing that was enough to survive until my first paycheck, since my rent and lunches would be covered by my school. But as your big sister here, I want you to set healthier money goals than I did in my younger years.

So a more responsible answer to the question all depends on:

◆ where you're going (what's the average nightly price of accommodations and food?)
◆ how you're traveling (bougie, budget, or balanced?)
◆ who you ask (your rich auntie who married her sugar daddy or your broke-ass cousin in college?)

One of the most helpful resources to determine where you can afford to travel based on your budget is NomadList.com. It compares safety, internet access, cost of living, and more, city by city all across the globe, and gives you the average monthly cost of living required to thrive there. These estimates are for slow travelers, not vacationers, but you can still use these estimates as a starting point for your travel budget.

According to Nomad List, the estimated monthly cost of living for a nomad who wants to live in Chiang Mai, Thailand, in 2023 is $1,303 USD per month ... but I say you can do it even cheaper if you forgo the gym membership and the co-working space membership. I say you can live in Chiang Mai for around $1,000 per month, which comes out to about $30 a day if you're slow traveling.

However, if you're going to Thailand on a tourist vacation,

are constantly on the move and want to stay in bougie hotels, visit the elephant sanctuaries, and take taxis everywhere, then maybe add an extra $350 (or more) on top of my estimate. Which still comes out to about $1,350 a month to be a backpacker or a tourist spending modestly.

Really, how much you spend comes down to how you like to travel.

I always say there are three ways to spend while you travel: budget, bougie, and balanced. Budget is staying in hostels and eating street food. Bougie is spending with the "You can't put a price on experiences" mindset. Balanced is somewhere in between.

I prefer the balanced route. Some nights I'll stay at a super simple guesthouse for $9 but splurge on a $45 food tour. Other days I'll spend $30 on a hotel and eat $1 street food. Sometimes I'll hunker down in an Airbnb for three weeks, cook at home, and go on little picnics. And then sometimes I know what my soul needs and I'll spend $400 on a three-day wellness retreat that includes all my food and massages and is a (relative) bargain that I hunted for! You'll find your balance. My advice is to start your calculations with accommodations and bucket list must-dos. How much will it cost to get a roof over your head? Food and adventures can be tweaked from there.

Pro tip: Use a travel budget app to track your daily spending. The app I love is called TravelSpend.

Moral of the story: Your travel budget can be customized to fit your wallet!

✈ **TRAVEL LESSON #11** ·······························

Slow travel = cheap travel.

Travel is considered slow travel when you're in a city for a week at the very least and living more like a local than a tourist. The longer you base yourself in one spot, the less expensive your cost of living becomes.

◆ You spend less on flights and buses because you're simply not moving around as much.

◆ You can invest in transportation cards, like the BTS Rabbit Card in Bangkok, which gives you a discount on metro fares.

◆ Instead of paying for nightly hotels, you rent weekly, monthly, or yearly — which costs much less. Even Airbnb gives weekly and monthly discounts.

◆ Most long-term rentals come with a kitchen, which means you can cook for yourself using local ingredients from affordable markets.

◆ You get to know the area, so you stop making expensive rookie mistakes.

Starting to see how this works? Where you travel and how slowly you travel really determine how much you're going to spend.

PS. I'd like to take this moment to throw some shade on the people who brag about traveling to every country in the world before they're thirty or forty or whatever. Fast travel is expensive, touristy, not environmentally friendly; usually doesn't benefit the local economy; and means that you haven't actually absorbed the culture of that country. And I swear to God, if I find out that you're counting touching down in an airport as "visiting" that country — then you're a damn cheater. Slow travel is cool. Fast travel is really, really lame.

ALEXA'S TRAVEL BUDGET HACKS

Once you've calculated your trip costs, it's time to save without excuses! You don't want to be one of those people who saves for twenty years for one single trip, right? So let's speed this process up, shall we?

Introducing the tricks, tips, and hacks that I've been using for the past ten years to manifest and manage my travel budget!

Hack #1: The Pad Thai Rule

One plate of pad thai in Thailand costs around $2 USD. Now, every time you spend $2, I want you to think, *That could buy me dinner in Thailand.* $10 at the movies? That's five dinners! $5 at Starbucks? That's two and a half dinners! Start counting your pennies because those pennies add up to a whole plate of dinner.

Even before you step into a foreign land filled with cheap street food, I want you to start thinking about your money as if you're already traveling. You're going to apply this rule to all spending that is nonessential. If you ever want to escape, you're going to have to change your spending habits at home. Start with these micro money changes:

◆ **Drink less.** You will not only spend less money on alcohol, but drunk you will no longer be online shopping at 10 PM on a Tuesday.
◆ **Have more gatherings at home.** Invite your friends over to cook and drink at home. The savings here are serious.
◆ **Cancel your gym membership.** Replace it with Chloe Ting's free workouts at home (check her out

on YouTube). Go outside. Run. Hike. Start replicating your yoga class in your living room.

Saving $730 a year means that you can afford enough pad thai to last you a year!

Please note: I have more respect for you than to tell you, "Stop buying coffee, and you'll be able to afford to travel." Buy the freaking coffee if you want, but at least do the math, see how much you're spending on coffee a week, and put yourself on a coffee budget.

Hack #2: Side-Hustle

Time is money, honey. If you've got any extra time whatsoever, start your Travel Path now by building a portfolio on a freelance platform like Upwork or Fiverr and start making money tomorrow. Chances are, you have skills that you could be monetizing right now! If you've got a computer, you've got an avenue to make some side cash. Got a car? My Lyft driver in Dallas was driving as a nighttime side hustle to save up for her van-life fund. Not only was she stacking that cash quickly, but she also shared her story with so many strangers that she had invites to park her van everywhere from Toronto to Todos Santos! So make your side hustle a game. Decide how much money you need to make in order to pay for that backpack and that flight — and then side-hustle that amount!

Hack #3: Follow Money Gurus on Social Media

Bombard your feed with money-mindset masters like Ramit Sethi (@ramit), author of *I Will Teach You to Be Rich*. Or follow Ajla Talks (@ajla_talks), my go-to finance girl on Instagram! She has brilliant money hacks for everything from travel to saving that my not-yet-fully-developed business brain can understand. Following her has changed the way I handle money. Here is an excerpt from one of her videos: "An extra $27.95 spent on daily things like coffee and lunch is $10,000 a year. Let that sink in." Add these little doses of money lessons into your daily life and watch your spending and saving habits improve.

Hack #4: Stop Hanging Out with Short-Term-Thinking Friends

This one sounds harsh, I know, but it's time to upgrade your social circle if you want to upgrade yourself. We all have one or a couple of "those friends" who hold us back from leveling up. The ones who don't spend money wisely, who party too much, who never set goals, who guilt-trip you into going out when you tell them you're trying to save money. I call those people "crabs in the bucket." Just as you're about to climb out, they grab you by the ankle and pull you back down into their dark, miserable life. Hang with big thinkers and doers instead.

Hack #5: Move Home

Whoa whoa whoa! Did I just say that? Yep, I did. If you have the luxury of belonging to parents who you get along with and who can afford to and are willing to house you, then take advantage of that massive money-saving opportunity, plus the extra time you get to spend with your family before you go.

If you're afraid that being thirty-five and moving home will make you look like a loser, I can assure you it won't. Every time you tell someone, "I moved home to save for my upcoming trip to Africa," you'll sound like a badass. If anything, this is a conversation starter!

PS. If you don't want to move home full-time, remember that you can always sprinkle house-sitting into the equation to keep from killing your parents. Murderers can't leave the country (legally).

If you're still stressing about saving money, let me leave you with this...

THERE IS BEAUTY IN BEING A BROKE BACKPACKER

As a broke backpacker, you don't have the option to take the easy route, so you take the interesting route. Instead of spending money on taxis, you walk your butt everywhere, becoming an expert in the cities you explore. You find the best street food, make friends with shopkeepers, take trains with locals, sleep on bus station floors, learn how to speak local languages, and learn to cook with local ingredients. Instead of going on food tours, you make your own food tours! You're forced to travel beneath the tourist surface. As a traveler on a budget, you enter worlds that fancy tourists will never discover.

And I'll tell ya, while staying at a luxury hotel, I've never had my night end around a table with beers and a shirtless Filipino dude playing the guitar. Sometimes fancy people miss out. Sometimes, when you're staying at posh hotels, you're choosing claw-foot bathtubs over wild stories. And sometimes that's okay. Sometimes I don't want to talk to anyone and would rather sprawl out in my expensive bed and order room service. Other times I want to drink moonshine with a suspicious couple from Florida who live on their boat in Panama.

As Emilia and I say, we go from the "Four Seasons to the Floor Seasons" and love them equally.

So set a money goal that's realistic for you. Be open to

roughing it if that's what it takes. Get creative with accommodations. Use the resources I've provided you. And be disciplined with hitting that goal.

Once you've saved up enough money to go, it is equally important that you know how to spend it correctly.

SPENDING LIKE A PRO

Half of the flights I took last year were free, and I haven't spent a dime on ATM fees since 2012. You're going to want to trust me on this next section.

When you book a trip, you're dropping some serious cash on flights, hotels, and gear. Then, while you're traveling, you're throwing cash around on ground transport, food, and shopping. A rookie traveler would let this drain their bank account, but an expert traveler would collect points for every dollar spent, which are converted to miles that equal free hotel stays and flights. They would also be sure they weren't being charged hundreds of dollars in ATM fees abroad (because that's a thing).

Before you spend a single penny on this trip, you need to have the right travel credit and debit cards.

What's in Alexa's Wallet?

I travel with two credit cards and two debit cards and carry them separately: one debit and credit card in one bag, the other debit and credit card in another bag. That way if you lose one set, you have a backup set.

◆   The credit cards are for booking everything before the trip, for spending during the trip, and also to have in case of emergencies like paying a hospital bill.

◆ The debit cards are for withdrawing local currency at ATMs to spend on everything at places that won't accept cards.

PS. Visa and Mastercard are accepted in nearly every corner of the world, while American Express is accepted less often by retailers outside the US simply because their processing fee is higher than Visa's or Mastercard's. I still carry my Amex and use it as my preferred card for online bookings, airport lounge access, and bougie establishments that accept it. But I usually use my Visa cards for day-to-day transactions.

Pro tip: Link your credit cards to Google Pay and/or Apple Wallet. This will allow you to skip the foreign exchange fees abroad — and fiddle with your physical wallet less.

Credit Cards 101

I grew up believing that credit cards were evil and would put me into debt. If you spend beyond your means and do not pay off your monthly balance, this is true. But if you use point-collecting cards, only buy what you can afford, and pay off your balance every month (I recommend setting up automatic payments linked to your bank accounts), then every time you spend, you are collecting points that let you travel for free. In that case, credit cards are not evil!

When you spend using a travel credit card, every dollar equals points, and those points add up to free flights, hotels, and flight upgrades! See those fancy people flying business class? Most of them did not pay cash for that upgrade; they used their points. If you want to fly fancy, that's how you do it.

Never use your debit card to book flights or hotels; use travel credit cards only.

The best time to order your travel cards is immediately.

Most travel credit cards have a sign-on bonus that awards you points after you spend a certain dollar amount within the first few months.

For example, at the time I got it, Capital One Venture X offered a sign-on bonus of 75,000 points after spending $3,000 within the first three months of getting that card. $3,000 is a lot of money, but I knew I had a trip coming up and I was going to spend at least $3,000 over three months, so before my trip was an opportune time to get this card. I booked everything on this card: my flights, hotels, travel insurance, a new backpack, and any other expenses (grocery store, hair salon, Hulu subscription) so I could hit that $3,000/75,000-point mark. I didn't quite hit it before I left, but I used my Capital One card as my main travel card in Cambodia to pay hotel and restaurant bills, and bingo! I unlocked my sign-on bonus by spending money I was going to spend anyway. My flight home was free, thanks to my 75,000-point bonus. Get it?

Pro tip: Want to hit that sign-on bonus but don't have justifiable expenses? Consider heading to Amazon, Target, Costco, or wherever you regularly shop and buying gift cards in the amount needed to unlock that bonus. Just make sure that the gift cards are valid forever and that you'll actually spend that money on necessities (not frivolous things). Only do this if you can comfortably pay off that $3,000 balance within your billing cycle. If not, buy the gift cards incrementally within the time needed to unlock the bonus.

With that said, don't overspend just to hit that mark, because then you're not "earning" points — you're buying them, and that doesn't make sense.

▶ Other Perks That Come with Travel Credit Cards

◆ TSA PreCheck and Global Entry (more on these in chapter 14)

- ◆ Airport lounge access around the world
- ◆ Flight cancellation coverage
- ◆ Purchase protection insurance
- ◆ And more game-changing things that more than jus-tify the yearly cost of these cards

▶ How to Find the Best Cards

To weaponize your wallet with the best travel credit cards, turn to Brian Kelly, aka the Points Guy (ThePointsGuy.com). He'll teach you how to earn and maximize your points to fly fancy and fly for free. Brian also has great advice on no-fee debit cards … which we need to discuss immediately!

Non-US Travel Credit Cards

Hey! I know that not all of you reading this are American — and so I have an international list of travel cards and travel perks on my website at Alexa-West.com/OneWay.

No-Fee Travel Debit Cards and ATMs

The first time I ever used an ATM in Cambodia, I was shocked by an $8 USD ATM fee. When a hostel dorm bed costs $4 for the night, $8 feels extreme! In addition to foreign ATMs charging you a service fee, your bank will likely charge you an additional fee for using an ATM outside their network. They feel like you're cheating on them, and they want revenge in the form of payment. Now you have two fees to pay when taking out cash while traveling, and those costs add up!

To avoid paying both fees, you need a travel debit card that (a) reimburses you for foreign ATM fees and (b) doesn't charge you fees to withdraw money. In other words, you need a card that lets you withdraw cash with no fees. The no-ATM-fee card I pledge my allegiance to is the Charles Schwab Visa Platinum Debit Card. They charge no ATM fees on their side and reimburse you 100 percent of any fees that foreign ATMs may charge you.

Foreign ATM Pro Tip

If an ATM in another country ever asks you if you would like to "accept" their "conversion," hit "decline conversion." Their conversion will cost you money, whereas if you decline their conversion, your own bank at home will do the conversion for you. Otherwise, you will essentially incur a double conversion and lose money. (By the way, the same is true when paying at a store or restaurant: when given the option to pay in your currency or the local currency via your credit or debit card, always choose to pay in the local currency and let your bank make the conversion.)

GETTING CASH IN ANOTHER COUNTRY: ATMS VS. MONEY EXCHANGE COUNTERS

Which is better: withdrawing cash from an ATM or bringing currency from home to exchange at a cash exchange counter abroad? Answer: You get the best exchange rate from an ATM. There are exceptions to every rule, of course, but when you use your debit card at an ATM, you are withdrawing money from your bank. Your bank is going to give you the "bank rate," aka the closest value to that currency.

Alternatively, when you exchange currency at a cash exchange counter, you may be subject to high exchange rates and fees, which can significantly reduce the value of your money. Especially in an airport. When possible, avoid airport exchange counters because they usually offer the worst exchange rate as they know you're a desperate prisoner (or an uneducated traveler) with no other options.

The only time I use an exchange counter is when my debit card isn't working. For that reason, I bring an emergency stash of cash. I usually travel with an extra $100 to $200 USD on any given trip but only exchange it if I really need it.

SPENDING CASH ABROAD

Before you spend, you need to learn the value of the currency. Sometimes foreign currency can feel like Monopoly money, but it's not! It's real cash that you worked hard to save. Before you hand over a bill, you need to know how much you're spending.

▶ *Three Ways to Convert Quickly*

1.   Memorize the rate. For example, I know that 100 Thai baht (THB) is *roughly* $3 USD. That's an easy conversion for me to remember.
2.   Download the currency conversion app XE. It's free.
3.   A fun trick: Write the rough conversion of each bill denomination on a piece of paper, like this:

1,000 THB = $30 USD
500 THB = $15 USD
100 THB = $3 USD
50 THB = $1.50 USD

And so on. Then, take a photo of this piece of paper and save that photo as your lock screen on your phone, and now you can glance down at the conversion quickly without having to open any apps. I recommend rounding the conversion up or down to the $.50 or $1 mark, whichever will make it easier for you to do math on the spot while haggling with a feisty merchant.

HOW TO HAGGLE

Haggling is a game. The goal of haggling is for both parties — the vendor and the shopper — to win. Know which countries play and where they play. Usually haggling is reserved for big outdoor or covered markets.

Let's say you go to a market in Thailand and find a dress you really like. If it doesn't have a price tag (or sometimes, even if it does), ask the vendor how much. If they are in the haggle game, here's what will happen:

They will tell you two to three times more than a reasonable price.

You will counter with around half that price.

You will settle on a middle ground between their initial offer and your counteroffer.

Like this:

You: How much?
Them: 200 baht.
You: Oh, okay, too expensive.
Them: How much do you want to pay?
You: 100 baht.
Them: *(Looking shocked)* I give to you for 160.
You: How about 120?

Them: Okay, 140.
You: Okay, 140.

Sometimes, you'll have to hang the dress back up and walk away. When you're walking away, they'll yell, "Okay, 120." You've got to be willing to walk away! That's the trick. But here is something important to remember: these vendors have to make a profit, too! Be fair. Don't be insulting with your prices, especially if the vendor is selling their own handicrafts. In that case, offering half the price might be a slap in the face, and so I'd aim for less of a "deal." Be kind. Smile your way through it. And if you love the dress that much, and they don't want to haggle, just pay the 200 baht.

KEY TAKEAWAYS

◆ Travel cards are a must. Get your travel cards before you buy your flights, hotels, or travel insurance to earn miles and get lounge access!

◆ ATMs usually offer better rates, but if you're exchanging money, try to exchange the majority of it in the city.

◆ Know the value of the currency and haggle fairly.

◆ Use NomadList.com to get an idea of how much money you should aim to save.

◆ Keep track of your spending now, starting with flights, and be diligent with tracking your spending as you travel.

CHAPTER 12

Trip Planning 101

Confession: I used to be an anti-planner. I thought travel guides and blogs were for tourists. I wanted to travel like a local, so I'd show up to a new country with an intense "go with the flow" mindset and have no idea what I was doing. In turn, I'd end up traveling like a tourist because I hadn't researched anything. I'd fall for the tourist traps, overspend, and miss out on incredible experiences that I didn't know existed off the beaten path.

Don't be like that. But also, don't be the person who travels with a strict hour-by-hour plan.

The biggest mistake I see people making while trip planning is trying to see everything in a short amount of time, thus overstuffing their itinerary. You wouldn't believe how many people come to me with plans to visit three countries in two weeks! Don't do this either!

Expert travel planning is all about striking a balance between having plans and having no plans. Leave space between activities. Plan to plan nothing in between your plans!

When you allow your itinerary space to surprise you, it will! When you meet other travelers you'll compare routes and share recommendations, like the phenomenal oysters your dormmate had in some tiny shack on the beach. Your trip will evolve as you go. Instead of having dinner at the hostel, you'll be in a *tuk-tuk* headed to search for those oysters down some sandy road after the second palm tree on the left. Because you left room for life!

So here is the secret to being a stress-free traveler: bucket list itineraries.

Bucket list + loose itinerary = Bucket list itinerary

Rather than a strict schedule, I create a rough list of what I want to do (my bucket list for that destination) and plan from there.

Nevertheless, I understand the desire for structure. Even I like to have some structure on some trips. So let me show you how I plan my trips from beginning to end.

▶ My Usual Planning Process

1. Organize your dreams.
2. Choose where and when to go.
3. Assemble your bucket list.
4. Make your timeline and create your route.
5. Book your flight(s).
6. Book your accommodations.
7. Book a few activities.

Sidenote for the Rebels.

You can always just book the flight first. If you come across an awesome deal that you can't refuse after a couple glasses of wine on a Tuesday on the couch...go for it! Be spontaneous if it feels right! Then come back to this chapter and follow the methods I'm about to teach you.

Disclaimer about my planning process: At any given time, I have ten destinations on my bucket list. I find joy in designing dream trips, even if it takes me five years to actually go on them. I literally have an entire Greece bucket list itinerary ready to execute, which I've had prepared since 2019. One day I'll use it.

That's how many of my dream trips are born, with a bucket list that grows until I'm ready to go. Sometimes, however, I have a very specific window of opportunity to travel and must plan a trip to match that window and weather. Both ways work.

The point being, don't get too hung up on the order of the steps I'm about to give you. Focus more on what I'm teaching you within each step. You can move the steps around to fit your trip, but if you're like me and have the entire world on your bucket list, this particular order may resonate with you best.

STEP 1: ORGANIZE YOUR DREAMS

I've got Pinterest boards for Greece, saved Instagram albums for Spain, and bookmark folders on my browser for road trips all over the US. Save your dreams in an organized manner that is easy to revisit when you're ready to make an itinerary. Plus, internet algorithms love to start showing you more Greece content once they see that you are interested in Greece, so use that to your advantage and start saving adventures when they cross your screen.

STEP 2: CHOOSE WHERE AND WHEN TO GO

Scuba diving took me to Thailand, waterfalls took me to the Philippines, and Angkor Wat took me to Cambodia. Every trip starts with a dream and evolves from there. But make sure that you're traveling when conditions are suitable to make your dream come true! You wouldn't believe the number of messages I've received over the years from travelers who arrive to Bali or Cambodia during the rainy season and are devastated that it's raining. *Like, you didn't look beforehand?*

There are a few factors you need to consider before you put a trip on your calendar:

1. **The weather:** Weather can affect your trip, especially if you're headed to a beach destination. In the rainy season, water conditions might not be ideal for snorkeling or diving. If the seas are too stormy, boats will stop running to small islands. So investigate whether the weather is going to hinder your ability to access your adventures. Find out if your destination has a hurricane season, a month of blistering heat, and so on.

   Only have time to visit during rainy season? Don't count that destination out! Rainy season can be magical! Trees are greener, waterfalls flow heavier, and thunderstorms are hypnotic. Plus, there are fewer crowds! I love to travel in rainy season and refer to it as "green season."

   If you're going for museums or temples, maybe weather won't matter. In that case, take advantage of visiting during "low season"...

2. **The tourist seasons**
   o **High season:** The best weather = higher prices and more people
   o **Low season:** Not the best weather = cheaper prices and fewer people
   o **Shoulder season:** The transition season between the two, and my favorite season to travel

3. **Budget:** Is your bank account ready for this particular destination at that particular time? Before you get your heart set on this trip, do a quick investigation on hotel and flight prices. You don't want to book a flight and then discover that hotels are more expensive than you anticipated. And you don't want to book a hotel only to learn that you can't afford a flight. So have a peek at both. Are flight prices reasonable? Are there hotels within your budget? Okay, you may proceed with planning. Are flights and hotels too expensive? Consider moving your dates to low season when prices are cheaper.

STEP 3: ASSEMBLE YOUR BUCKET LIST

Once I start to get serious about my trip, I begin organizing my ideas in an Excel or Google Sheets spreadsheet. With a spreadsheet, it's easy to copy and paste links to tours, addresses, or confirmation codes for hotel bookings and save activity ideas for when you're ready to book them. In other words, I make a mock-up itinerary first before I start booking anything.

Resources for Filling Up Your Bucket List Itinerary

◆ **GetYourGuide.com and Airbnb Experiences:** Book local tours with local people. I start researching every trip with these two websites, which cover must-do experiences. Even if I don't book their tours, I am able to quickly gauge what the most popular activities in that area are.

◆ **YouTube and blogs:** YouTube creators and bloggers deserve more credit! These people are explorers who create itineraries for you for free, including budget advice, transportation tips, and recommendations of lesser-known restaurants or areas that you might otherwise miss.

◆ **Guidebooks:** A good guidebook makes trip planning easy. It gives you a comprehensive breakdown of regions to visit, food to taste, and even routes to follow. In my guidebook series, The Solo Girl's Travel Guide, it's my goal to simplify the planning process by filtering out what's worth skipping and presenting only the must-sees. A highlighter and a guidebook are sometimes enough to plan your entire trip, starting with your bucket list.

◆ **Google Maps:** Pull up a city on Google Maps and browse restaurants, attractions, and spas. This wasn't always an obvious tool for me! Now it's my favorite way to find hidden gems. Use search words like "market" or "rooftop bar," and read through the reviews. Reviews are often so honest and stuffed with pro tips! Save these locations in Google Maps with the "Want to Go" flag, and revisit your map while you're on the ground exploring. When it's lunchtime and you're hungry, pull up your maps, and boom! You have a list of places you've already saved.

◆ **Free walking tours:** Almost every major city has free group tours led by enthusiastic locals on a donation basis. Tours can cover history, culture, food, or certain neighborhoods. Do a web search for "free walking tours" and the city you're visiting.

◆ **Hotel activities:** I stayed at a guesthouse in Kampot, Cambodia, that was right on the river. They had free kayaks, which is one of the reasons I booked with them. Activity planned! When you stay at social hostels, they often have a social calendar with events like river floating on Mondays and a pub crawl on Tuesdays. You don't have to stay at these hostels to join the activities either. You can just show up and join in.

- ◆ **Holidays and markets:** Chiang Mai, Thailand, has a Sunday market that, well, only happens on Sundays! Do a search to see if any special events or holidays will be happening when you're in town.

- ◆ **Personal hobby activities:** My last road trip around Baja Sur, Mexico, was essentially a scavenger hunt to visit pickleball courts and clubs that I had found on Google Maps. Bring your obsession, whether that's craft beer or open-mic nights, and see how the rest of the world nerds out on things you love. Beyond Google Maps, I search Facebook to see if there are groups that pertain to my hobby in the destination I'm visiting.

- ◆ **Recommendations from friends and family:** Just take these with a grain of salt. Your anime-obsessed cousin might have differing interests than you. Bonus points if you have friends of friends in your destination. Friends of friends have led me to concerts in parks, house parties with locals, and cafés in hidden alleys. Sometimes before a trip, I'll just post on social media and say, "Hey I'm going to Istanbul, does anyone have a friend there they can connect me with?"

10 Travel Things That Are NOT Cool Anymore

Leave these off your bucket list.

1. **Pictures with tigers.** These tigers are often drugged to pose for photos.
2. **Riding elephants.** This is pure animal cruelty.
3. **Running with the bulls in Spain.** Research what happens to the bulls after the event.
4. **Dolphins and whales in captivity.** Watch the documentary *Blackfish*.
5. **Instagram tourism.** Taking a photo but not experiencing the place.
6. **Volunteering at or visiting "orphanages."** Kids are not tourist attractions.
7. **Beg-packing or busking abroad.** Don't ask locals to pay for your travels in their country.
8. **Slum tourism.** Imagine someone coming into your neighborhood to take photos of how poor you were.
9. **Big cruises.** Large cruise ships can be an environmental nightmare. Because not only do they dump tons of waste into the ocean but also the ungodly number of passengers disembarking from these ships can contribute to overtourism and environmental damage. Small eco-cruises, however, can be lovely!
10. **Zoos and aquariums** that don't actively strive to be ethical. Animals in small cages? Not cool. Animals in sanctuaries or zoos that put the health and happiness of the animals first, above tourism? Better.

Ethical = Cool

Unethical = So not cool anymore (hint, hint to all the guys on Tinder with tiger photos and the girls with elephant-riding photos)

Here is a general rule of thumb: If you are considering any plans that involve animals, children, or underserved humans, do a Google search with the name of the activity, the place, and the word "ethical." If there is any controversy around this topic, this is a fast way to learn if you should move forward or swerve around accidentally funding harmful industries.

STEP 4: MAKE YOUR TIMELINE AND CREATE YOUR ROUTE

These two things happen at the same time. Like flipping pancakes while scrambling eggs, you'll go back and forth until everything is ready.

Make Your Timeline

Okay, so you've been obsessing over Cambodia with its beautiful white sand beaches and enchanting temples. You've watched some YouTube videos and read a guidebook while creating your bucket list, so you've got an idea of which cities you'll include in your route. Now you've got to figure out how much time you have to make it all happen.

Sometimes, no matter how long you *want* to stay, you're limited by how long you're *allowed* to stay, aka your "visa allowance."

When I plan a trip, I start by dreaming big. Then I narrow down my bucket list based on how long my schedule allows and/or my visa allowance. Let me explain.

Usually, travelers and backpackers enter a country on a tourist visa. How long do tourist visas last? That depends on the country. Many countries offer 30- to 90-day tourist visas, and other places, like Mexico, offer a 180-day visa! Some countries even allow you to extend your tourist visa. In Cambodia, for example, you can turn your 30-day visa into a 60-day visa with the help of a visa agency, which extends it for you.

Some countries, like Vietnam, require you to apply for your tourist visa beforehand (often online). Some countries allow you to just show up at the airport or the border and get your tourist visa as you arrive (this is called being "visa-exempt" or "visa-free"). The protocol all depends on the country you're visiting and your passport-issuing country.

Some passports have more power than others. Japanese citizens have the most powerful passport as of 2023; they can enter 193 countries visa-free. Afghanistan holds the weakest passport with just 23 visa-free entries. Western passports from the UK, the US, Canada, Australia, New Zealand, and Ireland are generally pretty powerful, and many countries allow these passport holders to enter visa-free. CIBTvisas.com is a helpful website for discovering visa allowances, aka how long you can stay where.

Create Your Route

Together, let's plan your quick hypothetical trip to Cambodia by matching your bucket list with your timeline to create your route.

You know that you have almost eight weeks to spend in Cambodia. Let's say you have a modest three things on your bucket list: to see Angkor Wat in Siem Reap, relax on the beach on Koh Rong, and sleep on the river in Kampot.

Ask yourself these two questions:

1. How many days do I need to do it all?
2. How will I get from place to place?

The answers will let you create your route, which at the most basic level, might look like this real-life itinerary I made for Cambodia:

Where	How long
Land at Phnom Penh airport — go directly to Kampot	5 nights
Train to Sihanoukville (2 hours) Boat to Koh Rong (45 minutes)	
The islands	2 weeks
Boat back to Sihanoukville (45 minutes) Overnight bus to Siem Reap (12 hours at 9 PM)	
Siem Reap	3 weeks
Bus from Siem Reap to Phnom Penh (6 hours)	
Phnom Penh	3 nights
Bus to Saigon, Vietnam (7 hours)	

In total, I only planned where I'd be forty-three nights out of fifty-six nights based on my bucket list for each destination. I gave myself wiggle room to go with the flow in case some epic opportunities popped up in between. And they did! Once I got to Kampot, I fell in love with my riverside bungalow. I had three empty nights in my itinerary, so I decided to stay in my bungalow a little longer.

It's so simple but so important to measure your time realistically, including the transport time and cost of transport between cities. In Southeast Asia, you can fly from Vietnam to Thailand in two hours for $40. But in South America, to get between Bolivia and Colombia, you might be looking at a $300 flight that takes twelve hours with a layover!

For this transportation between cities or countries, usually I recommend you book as you go. Don't limit your trip by having each bus and train and plane booked ahead of time, in case your travel plans evolve (which they often do). The exception: if you're going to be traveling during holidays, buy your tickets ahead of time (ground and air) and expect surge prices!

However, do research the routes ahead of time so you have an idea of how much you'll spend and how long each route takes. Use these sites to compare options:

◆ For ground transportation, I use 12Go.asia and Rome 2Rio.com.
◆ For flights, I prefer Skyscanner and Google Flights.

Pro tip: When booking ground transportation as you go, get advice at hostels and book your transportation through the hostels. Hostels cater to backpackers who utilize ground transport as if planes don't exist, and they tend to have all the nitty-gritty details of transport, including both budget and bougie options.

▶ Follow Other People's Routes

Planning to backpack more than one country? Go to Google Images and search for "Backpacking itinerary for X, Y, and Z." You'll often find route maps that backpackers have created. For example, in Southeast Asia it's common to backpack through Thailand, up into Laos, down into Cambodia, and over to Vietnam. You'll find maps detailing routes you can follow. You're not the first brave soul (usually) to explore this area, so don't be afraid to piggyback off someone who is knowledgeable enough that they took the time to map it out.

See if they've also indicated how long it takes to complete the route and how much money they spent.

▶ Want to Get Away from the Touristy Areas?

I always describe the solution to the overtourism problem like this: You know those mosquito lamps you can hang outside? The bright light lures all the mosquitoes to one location, and then the rest of the backyard is mosquito-free. The same goes for touristy areas. For instance, most people who come to Bali go straight to Canggu, Ubud, or Uluwatu, leaving the rest of the island for you to explore without the crowds. If anyone travels to Bali and says, "Bali is too touristy," that's because they travel like a tourist. To avoid touristy areas, don't travel like a tourist.

You can apply this to nearly every country. Instead of going to the most popular areas, go to the fifth-most-popular area, and then see if you can get off the beaten path from there.

▶ Want a More In-Depth Plan?

When it comes to ticking things off my bucket list in an organized fashion, I'll create itineraries for certain days that look like this:

Day 3: Siem Reap

AM:
>   Grab breakfast and coffee
>   Angkor Wat tour starts at 8 AM

PM:
>   Pool time at the hotel
>   Massage
>   Dinner
>   Bucket list of cocktail bars

Notice that my itinerary is broken down not by time but by AM and PM. This keeps me flexible.

Again, for both general and in-depth planning, I usually use a spreadsheet. You can access the One-Way Planner sheet for free by subscribing to my email newsletter on my website, Alexa-West.com.

Pro tip: Once you start making bookings, use the app called TripIt to organize everything you've booked. Just forward your booking confirmations to the app, and it arranges your bookings in a clean timeline, complete with booking confirmation numbers and hotel addresses.

STEP 5: BOOK YOUR FLIGHT(S)

Booking flights is an art form, and everyone has their own approach. Here's mine.

How to Find the Best Flights

Use Skyscanner, Kayak, or Google Flights to search flight routes. These websites will give you a list of flight options that let you compare prices, flight duration, and layovers.

Flexible with routes? Just need a vacation to any-freaking-where? In the destination slot on Skyscanner, type "everywhere." On Kayak, type "anywhere." On Google Flights, use the "explore destinations" function to see all the routes that depart from your airport, prices included.

Got some time between now and your departure date? Set flight alerts! Go on Google Flights, search for your route, and you'll see a little toggle button that says "set alerts." Until you turn it off, you will receive emails notifying you when that fare has gone up or down. See a good deal? Snag it.

Pro tip: If you're a frequent traveler, consider a subscription to Going.com (formerly Scott's Cheap Flights), which keeps you posted on the best flight deals on the internet, typically 40 to 90 percent off the average price for that route.

The key to getting the best deal is to be flexible with your departure date. Changing your flight by one day can save you hundreds! Use the calendar view function to see which dates have cheaper flights. Maybe Monday's flight is $100 cheaper than Tuesday's. That's a big win.

The Two *Smartest* Ways to Book Flights

Warning: Don't book your flight through third-party booking sites! These are sites with names like "BudgetSaver" that claim to offer you the lowest price on a flight or string of flights. Those flights may be cheaper (sometimes), but lord help you if you need to change your flight or seat or get a refund! Third-party travel agents like Travelocity sell you a ticket, but they do not have direct access to or control over your reservation.

For these reasons, I recommend you always and only book your flights in one of these two ways:

▶ *1. Book Directly on the Airlines' Websites*

◆ Create an account with each airline and start earning status when you book flights with your frequent-flier membership. This is how you get upgrades.

◆ Booking through the airline's website gives you access to customer service if your flight gets canceled or you need to reschedule.

◆ Book the wrong flight? Change your mind about your trip? You've got twenty-four hours to cancel flights that originate in or are going to the US! Under US federal law, airlines must allow customers to cancel their reservation without penalty within twenty-four hours of purchase for a full refund, as long as the flight was booked at least seven days in advance directly through the airline (or your credit card portal, which we'll talk about next).

Bonus to the 24-Hour Rule: Travel hackers use this rule to score the best flight deals. Learn more on this at Going.com/glossary/24-hour-rule.

▶ *2. Book with Points*

You can either book your flights directly through your credit card's travel portal or transfer your points to airlines' membership programs and get great deals. When I fly business class, it's usually by taking advantage of my points.

For example, Singapore Airlines has fantastic flight deals in their KrisFlyer program, so I always check their app before purchasing a flight. To fly from Cambodia to Seattle, I saw that I could book a flight for 60,000 points. I logged into my Chase.com account (linked to my Chase Sapphire Preferred credit card) and digitally transferred 60,000 of my points to KrisFlyer, just like transferring money from one bank account to another. A day later, 60,000 points appeared in my KrisFlyer account, and I was able to access their deal and book my flight without spending a penny (besides tax).

Pro tip for booking seats with points: KrisFlyer is run by Singapore Airlines and usually allows you to reserve your seat. But I used KrisFlyer to book a flight with a partner airline, EVA Air, which didn't allow me to book a seat online. So, after I had my confirmation number, I called EVA Air on the phone and selected the best seats possible through them.

So remember this trick if you use points to book a ticket with a partner airline and aren't able to select your seat when you book the flight.

Seat Selection

Since we're on the topic, let's talk about seat selection! For flights that are five hours or longer, I prefer a window seat so I can lean and sleep. Five hours or less means lesser chance of sleep and greater chance of drinking (especially on international flights, which offer free booze), so I choose an aisle seat because more beer means more potty breaks.

And if you've gotten the middle seat, well then, please rethink all your life choices. There is absolutely no reason for you to be in the middle seat! Save that seat for the people who didn't read this book! (Unless you're flying standby or you booked your flight last-minute — then you have a justified reason as to why you've denied yourself of elbow room.)

When to Book Your Flight

I once bought a ticket from Bali to Seattle twenty-four hours before the flight departed. The one-way ticket cost $800. As an experiment, I decided to track that route for an extra month to see how much the price changed. It went up, it went down, but it mostly stayed the same.

So while many experts might tell you that "Tuesday is the best day to shop for flights" and "booking a flight two months in advance will get you the best price" — I haven't found this to be the case lately. The pandemic and the emergence of the digital nomad population have upended conventional travel rules.

I spoke with a corporate travel expert to get their thoughts on the matter. They said that it used to be cheaper to fly during the middle of the week because business travelers would fly on Mondays and return on Fridays, while vacationers would fly on Fridays and return on Sundays. Both cases left midweek as the least busy time to travel, so airlines offered better fares. But now we have this rapidly emerging population of digital nomads who can fly any day of the week. Therefore, airlines are no longer struggling to fill midweek flights, so Tuesday through Thursday flights are no longer the absolutely cheapest days to book a flight. Book when you want!

So when is *really* the best time to book a flight?

▶ For Longer Flights

I'd say the sooner, the better. Start looking two to three months before your trip, if possible. Set Google Flight alerts. Give yourself some time to watch flight prices change, learn what "a good price" is for that route, and then book it.

▶ For Shorter Flights: Booking on the Go

When backpacking in Europe or Southeast Asia, however, buy short flights as you go. It's easy to find quick deals with budget airlines like Ryanair and AirAsia. And hey, you might discover that a bus or train between cities or countries makes more sense than a flight!

Layovers

Generally speaking, you never want a layover that is less than one and a half hours long. During a layover, you need time to get from gate to gate or terminal to terminal, make sure your bag gets from one plane to the other, and leave grace for flight delays. If you're switching airlines (like if you've booked two separate flights for one journey), then you will likely be required to collect your bags, clear Customs and Immigration, and start the whole check-in process again, including going through security. In that case, choose flights that give you a layover closer to two hours or more. And if you're flying back into the US from outside the US and transiting through a US airport before catching another flight to your home airport, you might even have to reclaim your bag, go through Customs, and check it again.

To recap on layover times:

♦ Generally speaking, an ideal layover is around one and a half hours long, especially if you're checking a bag.

♦ If you're flying internationally while checking a bag, changing airlines, or returning to the US after a trip abroad, layovers of two hours or more are best.

When I have a short layover, I do my best to carry my bag on instead of checking it — just to avoid the hassle.

▶ A Guide to Long Layovers

When I have a long layover, I make the most of it! Sometimes, I'll even choose a flight with a long layover just so I can leave the airport and explore. I recently had a nine-hour layover in Singapore and was able to leave the airport and grab dinner with a girlfriend in the city. *(Hey, Nadia!)*

Want to leave the airport? Consider:

♦ Does that destination offer you a visa-on-arrival (a visa that requires no preapproval) that allows you to leave for a couple hours, hassle-free? Or do you need to apply for a visa to leave the airport ahead of time?

- How far is the airport from the fun stuff?
- Remember that you'll need to go back through security when you return.

Pro Tips for Leaving the Airport

- Look for layover tours in your layover city. These are usually four- to eight-hour tours that include airport pickup and dropoff.
- Check out Dayuse.com, which lets you book hotel rooms for a few hours during the day at a cheaper rate than a full day.

Not leaving the airport? Enjoy lounge access! I try to convince anyone who will listen that airport lounges are a travel must! Please join my cult. Here's why:

- Interesting people hang out in airport lounges — make friends!
- Lounge food and drinks are free, unlimited — including water and alcohol!
- It's acceptable to drink alcohol at 7 AM as long as you're in an airport lounge. You leave buzzed and are no longer dreading your flight. Just don't party too hard. If you're wasted, you're not allowed on the plane.
- Some lounges have showers, massage chairs, and places to sleep.
- Free wifi means you can work during layovers.
- Some lounge memberships allow you to bring a buddy for free!

The best way to get access to lounge life is credit cards. Most travel credit cards give you access to the Priority Pass membership program, which is the key to lounge life around the world. Amex gives you access to the fancy Centurion Lounges *and* Priority Pass.

Justify it. Airport food is expensive! Airport water is expensive! So lounge life saves you money in the long run if you're a frequent flier.

If you don't have lounge access but have a layover, google "layover guide" for that airport! There are websites all about how to make the most out of layovers in airports all over the world, including the best places to sleep.

One-Way Tickets vs. Round-Trip Tickets

While I usually buy one-way tickets, I just bought a round-trip ticket to Baja California Sur from Seattle, and here's why:

◆ I know exactly how long I plan to stay in Baja.

◆ There is just one airport with direct flights to Seattle, so I definitely know where I'll be flying out of.

◆ I found a round-trip ticket from that airport for a good price.

Buy a round-trip ticket if it makes sense or gives you peace of mind! I, however, almost always buy a one-way ticket. Let me illustrate why.

My last trip to Vietnam was supposed to be from the north in Hanoi to the south in Saigon, but halfway through the trip, I decided that I wanted Thai food, so I flew to Thailand. If I had a set flight in Saigon, I wouldn't have been able to do that. Plans change. Don't limit your route by enforcing a fixed end point and end date.

The other piece of wisdom I want you to remember is that just because we wait for a good deal does not mean a good deal will come! Set a flight tracker, get an idea of the range of prices for that flight, and then just book it.

Starting to understand my booking advice? In terms of round-trip vs. one-way, this means:

♦ if you've got a one-week vacation and know your plan for sure — say, you're going to a wedding and then need to get back to work — buy a round-trip flight.

♦ if your plans are open-ended or you'll be moving between cities often, buy your second flight when you need it.

▶ Do You Need an Exit Ticket?

A big caveat here is that sometimes you will need proof of your exit flight before entering a country. Airlines and/or the country's Immigration department may want to see that you have an exit ticket out of their country. They want to know that you don't plan on disappearing into their society and staying forever. Sometimes the airline will ask to see your exit flight at the check-in counter before you board. Sometimes Immigration will ask when you land: "Proof of onward ticket, please."

This is such a buzzkill! You're being spontaneous! How are you supposed to know where you'll be in three months? However, the government is simply trying to prevent illegal immigration, so sometimes you're going to have to appease them.

To find out whether you need an exit ticket, check with the airline. See if they require an exit ticket. To save you some time, though, I can tell you that the UK, the US, Australia, New Zealand, Brazil, Costa Rica, Peru, the Philippines, and

Indonesia technically require an exit ticket if you're visiting as a tourist.

But sometimes, the airline personnel at the check-in counter don't ask for one. For example, when I enter Indonesia, I rarely have an onward ticket, and I'm rarely asked for one. Instead, when I land, the immigration officer asks how long I plan to stay. If my visa allows me thirty days, I tell them I'm leaving in thirty days. That's usually enough for them to wave me on through. Then, when I'm ready, I book my exit ticket to leave the country before thirty days.

Remember that you're not the only backpacker or traveler on a one-way ticket. You're a legit traveler and not an aspiring illegal immigrant, but you should still prepare to be asked about your onward travel plans.

▶ Tactics to Handle the Exit Ticket Conundrum

1. Remember that airlines originating from or going to the US offer a twenty-four-hour cancellation window. Buy a flight right before entering the country, then cancel it once you're in. Then you can buy a ticket that better suits you later.

2. Buy the cheapest ticket you can find to a neighboring country. Use it or don't.

3. Instead of an exit flight, buy an exit bus or train ticket out of the county. This is not official protocol, but immigration officers and airline personnel are human. If they see you have plans to leave the country, that might be enough to appease them.

4. Buy a round-trip ticket that allows you to change the dates for free. This will at least allow you some flexibility in your travel plans.

5. Google "best onward ticket" to discover another sneaky way to get around the one-way ticket dilemma. I'm totally *not* officially promoting this method, but I'm just here to tell you it exists...

6. If you're still super nervous, just buy a round-trip ticket for peace of mind.

Flight Changes and Ticket Cancellations

Once upon a time, I broke up with a guy and didn't want to sit next to him on a plane. So I needed to either change the dates of that flight or cancel that flight and book a new one later. I called the airline to see how they could help. If you find yourself in a similar position — or just have a change of plans — here's what you need to know!

▶ Changing Dates

Some tickets allow you to change the date once. Some allow you to change it an unlimited number of times. But often, especially when you've bought the cheapest fare available, changing a ticket can result in additional fees or a higher ticket price. Some airlines may offer a credit for the difference if the new fare is lower than the original fare, but this is not always the case. It's important to carefully review the terms and conditions of your ticket before making any changes and even before booking.

▶ Need to Cancel a Flight?

Airlines' cancellation policies vary depending on the type of ticket you purchased and the reason for the cancellation. Here are some general policies to be aware of:

Refundable vs. nonrefundable tickets: Refundable tickets are typically more expensive but allow for a full refund if you cancel your flight (regardless of whether you booked with cash or points), while nonrefundable tickets may only offer travel credits to be used within a year or two.

Timeframe for cancellation: Most US airlines will allow you to cancel your flight within twenty-four hours of booking without penalty. After that, you may be subject to cancellation fees or penalties.

Reason for cancellation: Some airlines may offer refunds or waive cancellation fees for certain reasons, such as a death in the family or a medical emergency.

Travel insurance: If you purchased travel insurance, it may cover certain cancellation fees or provide a full refund for certain reasons, such as illness or injury.

Worst-case scenario, if you cancel your flight more than twenty-four hours after purchase, you pay a fee anywhere from $25 to several hundred dollars, depending on the airline, the kind of ticket your purchased (economy vs. first class), and the fare.

But what if you don't feel like contacting the airline to cancel your flight? What if you just decide not to show up? Well, then expect a no-show fee, which can range from a small fee to the entire cost of the ticket. Trust me, it's best to let the airline know you're not coming.

Disclaimer: I have emptied my brain and given you all my extensive expert knowledge on flights, but please know that I am not Queen of the Sky. I cannot speak on behalf of every airline in every country, whose policies are always changing — this is just general information. So please, before you make any big purchase or changes, check the terms and conditions of your tickets and airlines.

STEP 6: BOOK YOUR ACCOMMODATIONS

✈ TRAVEL LESSON #12 ·······································

Where you stay will make or break your trip.

···

The staff, the location, the safety, the walkability, the social scene — your lodgings will set the tone for your entire experience, so pay extra attention to this section!

Hotels or Vacation Rentals?

As a solo female traveler, I like to stay in a hotel with reception so there's always someone to assist with questions, problems, or itineraries. However, I still check out Airbnb to see if there are any extra-special properties to consider, like an RV on the beach or a guesthouse with a Russian grandma who makes you breakfast from her garden. If the reviews mention that the host is super helpful, I'm more likely to consider that Airbnb.

Looking to travel slowly? Then I do prefer Airbnb for their weekly and monthly discounts. I'm looking at a place in Croatia right now where if you book for one month you get a 70 percent discount, taking the price from $2,300 to $700 a month! What a steal! Oh, and kitchens! When looking to rent a place for a week or more, a kitchen is a must if you want to cook or even heat up leftovers!

How I Choose My Hotels

First, I go on Booking.com and search by review score. Really simple! I use the sidebar to filter elements like budget, pool, bathtub, hostel vs. hotel, etc.

Then, I narrow down the selection by location! Location is everything, especially if you're alone. When possible, you want to be able to walk outside your door and feel safe exploring!

▶ *To Find the Best Location...*

1. Read the reviews. See what travelers have to say about the location.
2. Start with a landmark or a beach you want to visit, and find a hotel nearby.
3. Use the location filters in the sidebar that allow you to search based on the most popular neighborhoods.
4. Use map view. With map view, you'll also be able to zoom out and choose a hotel off the beaten path, away from the tourists, if you'd like. I love doing this. I once found a guesthouse in Cambodia only accessible by boat with a 9+ star rating. If I didn't use map view, I never would have found this place as it was in the middle of nowhere.

Booking pro tip: Before I book a place to stay, I put the name of the hotel in Google Maps and use the "walking" mode to get directions to the center of town to see if the location is practical. Walkability is everything!

▶ *Expert Booking Advice*

Cancellation policies: Book hotels with a free cancellation policy or a policy that allows you to change the dates if needed. Booking.com and Airbnb offer this on many properties, but not all.

Deals when booking direct: Hotel websites often offer deals that you can't find on third-party booking sites. Look for discounts as well as upgrades and packages that include massages, dinners, and excursions!

Travel hack: Book hotels via your credit card's travel portal and get points or benefits. Amex, for example, offers 5x points when you book hotels through their portal.

Scheduling: I like to leave gaps in between hotel stays. This allows me to extend a hotel stay that I'm enjoying and also discover new hotels along the way.

Hostel private rooms: Booking a private room at a hostel offers the best of both worlds: social opportunities and solo space. Sometimes, but not always, a room in a hostel can be cheaper than a room in a hotel. Alternatively, with trendy "poshtels" (posh hostels) or hostels that double as coworking spaces, a private room can be just as expensive (but sometimes just as nice) as a hotel. So find your top three hotels/hostels and compare based on price, location, and promised experience.

Small hotel tip: Small, boutique hotels book up faster than big hotels. Duh. Therefore, I tend to book small hotels farther in advance than big hotels. I don't want anyone stealing my room!

Boom. Now, you're a hotel pro.

STEP 7: BOOK A FEW ACTIVITIES

Once you've got a general idea of the flow of your trip, start making some reservations, but remember, don't overstuff your itinerary!

◆ Book an activity for your second day after landing. The first day is for acclimating, but the second day should be exciting!

◆ Food tours and walking tours are a brilliant way to begin your trip! You get the lay of the land and an introduction to local culture.

◆ Book seasonal tours and activities that are in high demand — like whale watching, which happens during the winter in Baja Sur but during the summer in Polynesia.

◆ Book things that tend to fill up fast, like a city's number one restaurant.

For flights, hotels, and activities, here is a summary of what to book ahead of time:

◆ Your first one-way flight (but not always your next)
◆ Your first few days of hotels
◆ At least half of your hotels for the rest of the trip, leaving a day between hotel bookings once in a while in case you want to extend or veer off the path for a few days
◆ Some tours and activities, especially if they're popular or bespoke
◆ The first five hours of your trip (which we'll cover in chapter 16)

Moral of the story: Stop planning every minute of your trip because guess what? Travel never goes as planned. Something is always late or early, and if you've got an hour-by-hour or even day-by-day regimen to adhere to, you're not going to enjoy the ride.

Whenever you think a country seems too intimidating, just remember that people explored it before smartphones and the internet. If they could do it then, you can certainly do it now. You could also forget this whole chapter, just show up, and wing it. Show up, talk to other travelers, get recommendations, and make it up as you go. You might miss out on some cool stuff, but you're sure to discover some cool stuff, too. This works even better if you have a guidebook in your hands (shameless plug for The Solo Girl's Travel Guide).

Meet me on my website at Alexa-West.com/OneWay when you're ready to start planning and booking.

CHAPTER 13

Packing

The saddest thing ever is watching a traveler struggle to drag a rolling suitcase through the sand across the beach. The second-saddest thing is watching a traveler carry their rolling suitcase above their head as they wade into the water, knee-deep, to get in an island-hopping boat. That being said, I will be a backpack traveler until the day I die!

✈ **TRAVEL LESSON #13** ·······································

Backpacks are better than rolling suitcases.

··

If you are going on a fly-and-flop vacation — where you land, go directly to the hotel, and stay there for your entire trip — a rolling suitcase is fine. But if you are really traveling and exploring, moving between cities and countries, then for the love of god, please take a backpack.

Me being me, I'd like to explain this to you with a story!

I heard whispers of this really epic resort located on a private beach deep in the jungle of Cambodia, so I did some digging and found the resort online. I messaged them and asked, "How do I get to you?" and they said that if I was traveling with a backpack, they'd come through the jungle on a motorbike and pick me up. If I had a rolling suitcase, then they couldn't get me. This is cold, hard evidence that traveling with a backpack is superior to traveling with a suitcase because with a backpack, you can go off the beaten path, you don't rely on sidewalks, and you don't need anyone to help you with your bags. The way I see it, rolling suitcases are for single-destination trips, and backpacks are for traveling.

Aren't backpacks heavy and uncomfortable to carry? you may ask. You should only be packing what you can carry. If it's too heavy, then you've packed too much. I am currently carrying around 17.5 kilos, which is about 38.5 pounds, and I'm totally comfortable because I invested in a proper travel backpack that fits my body and distributes weight evenly. I didn't blindly buy this backpack online. I went to REI (an outdoor store) and had one of their experts help me choose a backpack that fit my body. This is important! Get a backpack that fits your body, and you'll be fine walking around Nepal like a happy little turtle. I recommend you get a backpack that holds between 40 and 55 liters. Any bigger is inconvenient to travel with unless you've hired a sherpa to follow you around 24/7.

Don't have the chance to visit an outdoor store? I highly recommend you look into Osprey backpacks. Most female travelers I know use them. On their website, Osprey.com, you can find which backpack will fit you best. Osprey also makes hybrid bags that are essentially backpacks with wheels — if you want to compromise.

CARRY-ON OR CHECK?

I always prefer to carry on my bag for a speedy exit out of the airport and less chance of losing my bag! Plus, some airlines charge extra for checked bags. So let this be your motivation to pack light and go for luggage that is carry-on approved (usually 22″ x 14″ x 9″, but it varies a bit from airline to airline). When you're shopping for carry-on bags, usually they are labeled as "carry-on." Easy. However, my 55-liter Osprey Fairview bag is technically bigger than the carry-on allowance, but I pack it in a way to make it look slim instead of bulky so that (a) no one questions me about it and (b) it actually fits in the overhead compartment.

Another thing to consider: weight. Both your checked bag and carry-on bag have a weight allowance. When checking a bag, you cannot exceed that weight. When carrying on a bag, however, you sometimes have the opportunity to be sneaky. The airline attendant may not weigh it. It's a gamble. My theory is that when your bag looks less like a big heavy mess, the airline attendants are less likely to ask you to weigh it — depending on location and airline, of course.

Tips for Checking a Bag

- If you do check a bag, lock it with a TSA-compliant lock during transit.
- Consider attaching or sewing luggage trackers (little tracking devices) into your checked bags so you can locate them if you lose them.
- Never check valuables like jewelry, electronics, or money. Carry your valuables with you.
- Treat your personal carry-on bag like an emergency weekend bag, packed with an extra outfit, toothbrush, and toiletries. This way, if your luggage gets lost, you have some items to hold you over until it's found.

WHAT NOT TO PACK

How much stuff do you need to be happy, safe, and comfortable while traveling? Not a lot.

How much stuff do you need to be a total pain in the ass while traveling? Also, not a lot.

Over-packing will make you miserable and immobile, while under-packing is solvable nearly everywhere in the world. Really, you can find shampoo, rain ponchos, and USB cords at the most random roadside stands in the middle of Timbuktu. So stop anxiety shopping! Take all the things you think you need to pack and cut that in half! I swear to you, you will be thankful that you left space in your bag for shopping and collecting trinkets from around the world because when someone asks you, "Where'd you get that necklace?" it's so fun to say, "Oh, this ol' thang? I got it in Tanzania." Let the world be your market!

▶ To Pack a Book or Not Pack a Book?

I always pack at least one physical book on every trip and rely on audiobooks for the rest of my travels. There's just something about having a physical book to keep you company on the plane or make you feel a little less lonely at a café. When you finish that book, look for bookstores or hostels that do book trades — because depending on where you're traveling, it may be difficult to find books that you're interested in in your language.

WHAT TO PACK — THE ESSENTIALS

What you're going to carry totally depends on where you're going and when. If you're going to volunteer at a school in Nepal, you're going to need a more conservative wardrobe with breathable fabrics that let you sweat. If you're going to Mexico City in the fall, you're going to need a very confusing wardrobe because the temperature changes from warm to cold hour by hour. In that case, bring a day purse that can fit your sweater.

Packing is an art form. Consider these three elements while packing:

1. **Weather:** Will you need a light rain jacket or copious amounts of sunscreen?
2. **Activity:** What kind of shoes should you pack for a trip that includes both cave trekking and rooftop bars?
3. **Culture:** Is it totally inappropriate for your cleavage to be exposed? Do you need to cover your knees?

Then pack modestly to create...

A Capsule Clothing Collection

You do not need thirty outfits for thirty days. You need a minimalist collection of clothing that can be mixed and matched, dressed up or dressed down, and layered to create different looks. With this method, I'm able to easily pack two to three months' worth of wardrobe into one travel backpack. The fashionistas of the world call this a "capsule collection."

My capsule collection always includes:

◆ bathing suits that I also wear as bodysuits
◆ leggings for travel days and hiking days, which can be dressed up or down
◆ cardigans or front-tie sweaters to transform summertime sleeveless dresses into chilly airplane outfits or temple-appropriate garb

♦ wrap skirts and dresses that cover my knees for temples and conservative events

This collection doesn't have to be expensive, but don't waste your money on fast-fashion pieces that aren't durable enough for travel. Buy pieces that will stand the test of time and will save money in the long run. Here are some tips to nail your capsule collection.

♦ **Consider activewear as travel wear.** Activewear materials are moisture wicking, breathable, and wrinkle resistant. An active dress with built-in shorts that doesn't require a bra is my favorite thing to wear while traveling! I also love tennis skirts and active tops that I can hike in *and* go out dancing in. It's all about the multipurpose outfits!

♦ **Carry travel-friendly fabrics.** Yes, linen and cotton are breathable, but holy crap, do they wrinkle! I prefer low-maintenance materials that I don't have to iron! Synthetic fabrics like polyester, spandex, nylon, and rayon are easy to throw in a bag and go. They are wrinkle resistant and quick drying! They are also often more durable than natural fibers like cotton or wool, which can be prone to shrinking or stretching. If you prefer natural fibers, consider materials like merino wool or bamboo. Merino wool is soft, breathable, and odor resistant, making it a great choice for cold-weather packing. Bamboo is also a good option as it is lightweight, moisture wicking, and eco-friendly.

♦ **Bring the right jacket(s).** When shopping for rain jackets, know that "water-resistant" jackets are meant for light rain over a short period of time. They have a coating that repels water. "Waterproof" jackets are made with material that is completely impervious to water. If you're looking for something to keep you warm without the bulk, go for a light down jacket, which is easy to compress and pack.

◆ **Rollable and compactable are key.** When I buy jackets or sweaters, I practice rolling them to ensure they won't take up too much space, and I pack them using my double-zipper compression bags…

Packing Cubes?

To organize your belongings, you don't want vacuum-sealed bags. Those aren't practical on the go. Instead, I use compression bags with two zippers. One zipper closes the bag. The second zipper condenses the bag, squeezing all the empty space out. Easy to unpack and repack! You can see the exact compression bags I use in my travel store at Alexa-West.com.

Pro Tip: Be Ready to Do Your Own Laundry

Imagine sending your favorite flowy dress to the laundry lady only to have it returned with a big fat Regina George nipple hole! Devastating! Don't trust the laundry lady with anything irreplaceable. I now travel with these little laundry detergent sheets that foam up perfectly in the sink. Or for a better value, bring a one- to three-ounce bottle of laundry detergent to wash your clothes in the sink or bathtub. When I do decide to trust the laundry lady, I still don't give her my irreplaceables, and I ask her to hang-dry my clothing if the weather permits.

Shoes

I am not a minimalist at heart. I dream of having an extravagant walk-in closet with a floor-to-ceiling shelf for my shoes. Yet, when I travel, I only bring three pairs of shoes: running shoes (for pickleball and hikes), slide sandals for lazy days, and either walking sandals or warm boots that I can dress up or down, depending on the weather.

Have a size 9 shoe in the US or size 40 in Europe? Totally normal. Have a size 9 shoe in Asia? You are an ogre woman with hooves that shake the earth when you walk. If your shoe size is above a US 9 (or your clothing size is above a large), know that you might have trouble finding your sizes if you travel to lands where women tend to be petite. In this case, bring quality essentials that you won't need to replace.

Toiletries

▶ *Nonnegotiable Toiletries*

- **Damage-repair shampoo and conditioner** or something equally nourishing after exposure to heat and salt water
- **Reef-safe sunscreen**. Sunscreen is expensive in less-developed parts of the world (because only us travelers really use it), and very rarely will you find reef-safe sunscreen that won't poison the marine life where you're swimming or snorkeling. Bring your sunscreen!
- **A tinted moisturizer with SPF** for the face (rather than foundation)
- **A face serum for day and a hydrating night cream**
- **Body lotion or aloe vera**

Pro tip: Any time you get a sample of shampoo or moisturizer, save it for travel!

▶ Period Preparations

Ditch the tampons. They waste space, are not eco-friendly, and depending on the culture, may be hard to find. Better idea: switch to a menstrual cup before you travel. Test out a few menstrual cups and see which works best for your body. It takes about three menstrual cycles to master using the cup. Stick with it!

Have you ever used period-absorbing panties? I wear those along with my menstrual cup on travel days when I am being active or will be stuck on a bus for a long time. I get paranoid about leaks.

Last period tip: download a period-tracking app so you won't have any surprises on a catamaran in the middle of the ocean on a swimsuit day.

Don't Pack Illegal Things

Don't pull a Brittney Griner, forget to remove your cannabis oil from your bag, and end up in a foreign prison. Know what is legal and illegal to carry. Double-check your bags and pockets before you head to the airport!

▶ Makeup and Hair Care

I've met women who think that the less makeup you wear, the more hard-core of a traveler you are. I say, screw that! My makeup time is my morning "me time." But when I travel, this "me time" is much quicker. I keep my makeup bag small, and I leave a little room because it is so fun discovering new beauty products around the world.

In my travel makeup bag, I carry a tinted moisturizer, tinted lip balm, waterproof mascara, and a bronzer/highlighter palette that I can use on my cheeks and eyes.

Pro tip: Carry a plastic eyelash curler rather than a metal one because if your metal eyelash curler bends in transit, you risk chopping off your eyelashes. Or do what I do and plan to get an eyelash lift and tint wherever you're going. Now, no mascara or curler needed.

Let's talk hair! Prepare your hair to survive depending on the environment! Sunny? Bring a leave-in conditioner. Going to be in the ocean often? Bring a detangling comb. Going to humid weather? Forget the hair curler. Your hair won't hold that curl, and instead, your style will be braids and ponytails! Super cold weather? That's actually great for your hair, but if you plan on bringing any electric hair tools with you, check that the voltage of the destination is compatible with your tools so you don't blow a fuse.

The best thing you can do for your hair while traveling is to bring a high-quality sulfate- and paraben-free shampoo and conditioner with you, a wet brush to use in the shower, and a leave-in conditioner that protects against heat. Don't try to get fancy with your hair — it's a losing battle, especially for backpackers.

FUNNEST PACKING TIP OF ALL

With so many pockets and zippers, it's easy not only to lose track of where you've put things, but also to have a panic attack thinking you've lost your passport.

So here is what you're going to do: As you're packing,

pick where things will live. You're going to give your items a home and declare each item's residency out loud, like this:

- "My passport lives in the front zipper pocket of my fanny pack."
- "My earbuds live in the inside pocket of my laptop bag."
- "My deodorant lives in my makeup bag." (Really, keep your deodorant here. You'll never forget to put it on.)

Say these things out loud, and watch how well your brain remembers where to locate what you need!

DON'T KNOW IF YOU'VE PACKED TOO MUCH? THREE TIPS!

Tip 1: Pack your bag. Leave it alone for a day. Then go back to it and take out two things you're not sure you'll need. Removing those two things will make a difference.

Tip 2: Practice walking with your bag up a set of stairs. If it feels too heavy now, then it's certainly going to feel too heavy while you're traveling. Do yourself a favor and take some items out to make your bag less of a burden.

Tip 3: Confirm your luggage weight allowance in accordance with your flight reservation and then weigh your bag before you go to the airport. Overage fees suck.

I promise you, packing for this trip is way simpler than you think. I have free no-bullshit packing lists for you on my website that will help you pack for different climates and Travel Paths. Go to Alexa-West.com/OneWay.

Travel Planning Action

Explore your closet before you start shopping! Build your own capsule travel wardrobe with versatile items you love and feel comfy in already.

Last thing to note: I've never heard someone say, "I wish I'd packed more things." But I'll tell you what I have done. I've abandoned an expensive rain jacket in a hotel in Bolivia because I didn't want to carry something I never used. I've put a collection of tiny new skincare bottles on the doorstep of a girl my age in a village in Bulgaria. I've given things away all around the world — things I thought I needed but never actually used. I've never thought, *Dang, I should have brought those jeans or that dress.* In fact, I've only thought, *Dang, why did I bring all this crap?*

CHAPTER 14

Prepping

This is all the stuff you need to *do* before your trip! Most of these processes are easier to complete with website links and tutorials, so when it's time for you to prep, meet me at Alexa-West.com/OneWay. But since you bought this book, let me give you your money's worth with some expert prepping guidance right now that will give you a substantial head start.

▶ *Your Pre-departure To-Do List*

❑ Vaccinations
❑ Visa(s)
❑ Travel insurance
❑ Bank cards and cash
❑ Journal
❑ International driver's license (if you want it)
❑ Beauty and medical prep
❑ Birth control and prescription medication
❑ Internet and data on your phone
❑ Maps, apps, and VPN
❑ The emergency stuff
❑ Homesickness insurance

TSA PreCheck, Clear, and Global Entry

For my American friends: Having TSA PreCheck, Clear, or Global Entry status will make your entire process through airport security and Immigration much quicker and smoother. But it requires advance planning and can take weeks or months. Research the programs to figure out which is best for you, and apply well before your trip. And keep in mind that many travel credit cards include these perks!

Let's break these down.

VACCINATIONS

The specific vaccinations required or recommended for international travel vary depending on a number of factors, including the traveler's age, health status, destination, and the activities planned. But here are the most standard vaccinations to consider:

- MMR (measles, mumps, rubella)
- Tetanus or Tdap (the combo vaccine that covers tetanus, diphtheria, and pertussis)
- Hepatitis A
- Hepatitis B
- Influenza
- Typhoid fever
- Covid-19 (as I write this, more and more countries are relaxing this requirement, so please check with your airline or your destination's official government website to see whether you have to present proof of vaccination)

Beyond this list, you may need other vaccines and medications, depending on which region you're traveling to. For example, yellow fever vaccination is required for entry into some countries in Africa and South America.

▶ Which Vaccinations Do You Need?

To find out which vaccines are mandatory or recommended for your travels, check the embassy or consulate website of the country you plan to visit. They list the most up-to-date vaccination requirements and entry regulations. You can also refer to the Centers for Disease Control and Prevention (CDC) website, which provides updated information on recommended vaccinations for international travel, as well as alerts and notices for disease outbreaks in different parts of the world. However, not all vaccinations or medications listed on the CDC website are mandatory. Some are just recommendations to help you prevent potential health issues while traveling. For example, the CDC recommends the rabies vaccine and malaria medication when traveling to Cambodia, but these are not mandatory or even that common among Cambodia travelers. Before you jab up your body and spend a bunch of money, it's important to speak with a healthcare provider or a trusted source to determine which precautions are necessary and right for your trip, based on your individual health needs and travel itinerary.

▶ Money-Saving Tip

The last time I was due for some shots, they were expensive in the US, so I waited and got them for a third of the price at a hospital in Bangkok that was recommended to me in a Bangkok expat Facebook group.

VISA(S)

Don't be the person who takes a bus to Vietnam only to be denied entry at the border because you didn't realize that you had to apply for a visa before arrival! Research the country or countries you're visiting to determine whether you'll need to apply for a visa beforehand. More about this in chapter 17.

TRAVEL INSURANCE

Do you really need travel insurance? Yes, yes, you do.

✈ **TRAVEL LESSON #14** ·····································

Do not travel without travel insurance.

···

From the big accidents to the weird stuff your body might do at any given time, travel insurance is a must in my (literal) book. Not only can travel insurance cover sickness and medical emergencies, but it also can offer protection for lost luggage and canceled flights. This is one of those "better to have it and not need it than to need it and not have it" situations. Traveling with insurance isn't usually a legal requirement; rather, this is just my personal and professional advice.

The type of insurance you need will vary depending on the nature of your trip. Are you going to Paris to eat croissants and sip wine? Then a standard travel insurance plan will likely work for you. Are you going to climb a mountain in New Zealand and then paraglide off it? Then you need to find an insurance plan that covers more extreme activities. Each insurance plan will have a list of what it covers and what it does not cover. Before embarking on your journey, always ensure that your intended activities are included in your chosen coverage.

When it comes to paying for covered expenses, different insurance companies have varying payment procedures. Some may directly pay for your emergency expenses, while others may require you to first pay out of pocket and then file a claim for reimbursement. This highlights the importance of having a travel credit card, as it can be used to cover unexpected accidents or delays, preventing a dent in your travel budget or issues with paying hospital bills. Make sure to collect detailed documentation of your medical visits, such as itemized lists and receipts, to facilitate a smooth claims procedure. I know, I know. This is a lot to process, so meet me on my website at Alexa-West.com/OneWay, and I'll walk you through finding the right insurance for your needs.

BANK CARDS AND CASH

Done and done. We've covered cards in chapters 11 and 12. You know what to do. *Look at you, an expert already.*

JOURNAL

At all times, I carry a little purse-size journal with me. A company called Paperage makes a 3.7-by-5.6-inch journal that is so travel-friendly. I designate half of the journal for stories and thoughts and "morning pages," which is a ritual that both Emilia and I have committed to where we write three pages of anything that spills out of our heart and head every morning. Three pages minimum! The other half of the journal is for things I want to recall, like how to say a phrase in another language, or for tiny moments I want to remember, where I'll write something simple like "Raven, girl with a face tattoo that I met on the train."

INTERNATIONAL DRIVER'S LICENSE

If you plan to drive a car abroad, get an international driver's license. For Americans, go to AAA Travel, where an international license costs $20 USD and is valid for one year. British drivers, you can obtain an international driver's license through the post office or the Automobile Association (AA). Wherever you're from, do a quick search online and see how you can obtain yours. Usually, there is no test needed. An international driver's license is simply an extension of your existing driver's license.

If you have a motorbike license at home, get it translated into an international license by following the same process outlined above. Otherwise, you can look into getting a motorbike license in the country you're traveling to (if your visa permits you to apply) or you can do what most travelers do, which is to ride without a license. If you do this, you risk getting fined if stopped by police, and you will have to pay out of pocket if you get in an accident. If you can avoid riding a motorbike, avoid riding a motorbike.

BEAUTY AND MEDICAL PREP

Most girls get waxed and get their nails done before they travel, but no, no — they're doing it all wrong! Embrace beauty tourism and medical tourism!

I fly to Puerto Vallarta, Mexico, from Seattle just to get my hair done by a local guy who is an absolute blonde artist, and he's $100 cheaper than Seattle salons. So I fly down, have a mini-vacation, and get my hair done. I also get my teeth cleaned, go to the gynecologist, get my Botox, get waxed, get my nails done, and have a spa day. This is called beauty tourism and medical tourism! I find my beauty and medical tourism hotspots mostly through scrolling local Facebook groups for girls, Google Maps, Tripadvisor, and Instagram. Not only is it a dollar saver, but it's also a chance to enter another layer of local life. Hanging in the nail salon with the local ladies in Cuba is one of my favorite memories of that country!

Are you teaching or working in another country and have a legal visa? Then that visa might come with health insurance, which is how I got my chipped front tooth fixed for $5 USD in Taiwan!

Waxing heads-up: You need two or three days after waxing before going in salt water. If you're headed straight to the beach from the airport, go ahead and get waxed at home before you fly.

Before you travel, do some research and see if there is a highly rated hair salon or brow studio near your destination. Add it to your bucket list and make appointments! If not, go ahead and get these services done at home before you fly.

BIRTH CONTROL AND PRESCRIPTION MEDICATION

Revisit chapter 8 for my big-sister birth control advice and make your birth control plan before you go.

When it comes to medication, you need to know two things. First, your prescription from your home country will most likely not work at a pharmacy overseas. If you will need a medicine refilled abroad, check to see if you can get it over the counter where you're going, as many countries have more relaxed prescription rules than the West. Also be sure to check whether that medication is even available where you're going. If it's not, consult with your doctor to see if you can find the equivalent medication for that destination.

Second, understand that just because your ADHD medication is legal in the US does not mean that it is legal abroad. Narcotics, sedatives, or amphetamines are highly regulated in some countries, so you run the risk of your medication being confiscated or worse, facing a fine or jail time if it's flagged as illegal. To avoid this, check with your embassy for a list of medications that your destination country allows or regulates. To avoid hassle, always keep your medications and even vitamins in their original bottles with their prescriptions and labels.

▶ *Pro Tip: Ask Other Expats*

Recently, a girl in my "Girls in Bali" Facebook group was having a hard time finding out how to bring her ADHD medications to Bali, since they're technically illegal. Confused by all the information online, she asked if anyone had any experience bringing this medication — and the answers she received were phenomenal. Other expats had been through the same stress and were able to offer her advice.

Here's what we learned: She could bring a "personal supply" of that restricted medication as long as it was in the labeled prescription bottle and she traveled with a doctor's note. She would also have to "declare" this medication upon landing in Bali.

You are not the first person to have this question. So ask for answers in forums, but then cross-check the answers with your doctor, a visa agency, or your embassy.

INTERNET AND DATA ON YOUR PHONE

Right now, in your phone, you've got a little chip called a SIM card. If you're with Verizon, it's a Verizon SIM. If you're with

T-Mobile, it's a T-Mobile SIM. This SIM gives your phone data or internet. But when you fly to another country, you might not be able to use that SIM.

So how do you get reliable internet on your phone when traveling? Obviously, you can connect to wifi, but just know that wifi does not enable you to text your mom at home. To text her on wifi, you need a messaging and calling app like WhatsApp or Skype. Or if you have an iPhone, you can use iMessage with a wifi connection. If there's no wifi, you'll need data.

Three Ways to Get Data on Your Phone

Option 1: Get an international plan with your phone carrier. But watch out! This can get expensive! Like $10 a day expensive!

Option 2: If you travel between the US and other nations often, consider ditching Verizon, T-Mobile, or AT&T and switching carriers to GoogleFi, which offers the best coverage all over the world for the best price.

Option 3: Often local data plans are cheaper and more reliable than international plans. And often, but not always, you'll need a local SIM to use local apps. So, when you land, purchase a local SIM card. Additionally, having a local phone number can be useful for making local calls and receiving texts.

Where to Get a Local SIM

Airports almost always have a kiosk with local SIM cards in the arrival hall, after Customs. Sometimes the airport SIM cards are slightly more expensive than if you were to wait and buy a SIM card at a cellphone store in the city. However, I prefer to pay what I call a "convenience fee" just to leave the airport with a phone connected to data.

A Few More Savvy Phone Tips

♦ Switching SIM cards? Those things are tiny and easy to lose. Designate a pocket with a zipper for SIM cards.

♦ Buying a new phone? Buy a phone with a "dual SIM." This allows you to carry two SIM cards in one device and switch between them. Or purchase one with eSIMs, which don't require a physical SIM. The world is shifting to eSIMs already. Just be sure that your phone allows for two eSIMs at one time so you can keep your home number and use a local number, if you wish.

♦ Check that your phone is "unlocked," which means that your phone isn't locked to just one data provider. If your phone is locked, you may be able to contact your carrier and request an unlock code. Some carriers may charge a fee for unlocking your phone, while others may unlock it for free after a certain period of time. Once your phone is unlocked, you will be able to use a local SIM card when you travel.

♦ When buying a local SIM, always ask the clerk to assist you in setting up your SIM card, and don't leave until you can confirm your data is working — because lord help you if you are left to set up your data plan alone in a foreign language!

What I Do for Data

I use GoogleFi *and* buy a local SIM when I land. GoogleFi lets me keep my US phone number, which I often need to receive verification codes when my bank or my email suspects a suspicious login. But I also need the local SIM to use rideshare and food delivery apps.

I also pay a yearly fee for a Skype number. This is a phone number through the Skype app that lets me call landlines (like airlines) and cell numbers. The app also lets people call me no matter where I am in the world just like a regular phone number. My Skype number never changes, so I use it as my contact number for my email, apps, and so on because it usually accepts SMS codes in the app — but not always. Best of all, no local SIM needed. You can use Skype with wifi.

Summary: I travel with both my GoogleFi number and my Skype number. And when I need to use local apps, I get a local SIM card.

MAPS, APPS, AND VPN

These days, travel apps make travel a whole lot easier and more accessible. You're never alone when you have a phone!

Maps

Download Google Maps of your destination(s) *before* you travel there so you can access them when you might not have wifi or data.

Step 1: While on wifi, search the city you want to download, or zoom in on the area you're going to.

Step 2: Type "OK maps" into the search box and press enter.

Step 3: You'll be prompted to download the map so you can access it offline.

Step 4: Voilà! Explore with Maps offline.

For a tutorial on how to do this, visit my "Travel Tips" Instagram highlight @SoloGirlsTravelGuide.

Not a Google Maps fan? Find another map app you love, like Maplets, which lets you download maps of cities, hiking trails, and even airports.

Apps

▶ *Local Apps*

I met a guy who had been traveling in Cambodia for weeks and didn't know about PassApp, the most popular rideshare app in Cambodia! So take a minute and do some googling to find the most popular apps for your destination country, like their rideshare apps, texting apps, and food delivery apps. As mentioned earlier, you will likely need a local SIM to use these apps. Know before you go.

▶ *Entertainment Apps*

Download your audiobooks and offline playlists with Audible, Libby, Spotify, etc.

▶ *Travel Apps*

Download TripIt, the organizing app, and TravelSpend, the budgeting app. Also, download the apps for the sites you've used to book your accommodations, like Booking.com or Airbnb. Having the app ensures that you'll have quick access to the chat feature, confirmation codes, and addresses.

▶ *Safety Apps*

◆ To share my location with family and friends 24/7, I use the Google Maps "share location" feature. This is free.

- For temporary sharing, you can send someone your live location through WhatsApp for up to eight hours or send them a one-time location.

- To share your location with authorities in an emergency, download TripWhistle or use the iPhone's SOS feature, which allows you to share your exact coordinates for the next time you're lost in the woods or something.

- Want a super-tracker app? The free app called Life360 not only tracks your live location but will send alerts to the people you've chosen to add in your "circle" when your phone battery is low and keeps a history of your trips and routes. So you really need to be comfortable with the people you include in your Life360 circle because they will know everything about you!

VPN

A friend who checked his bank account online in Indonesia via an unsecure wifi network had his account drained. A VPN (virtual private network) can provide an extra layer of security when accessing the internet, particularly on public wifi networks or even hotel networks. It encrypts the internet connection and routes it through a remote server, which can help protect your online activity from potential threats, especially while traveling.

I usually use NordVPN. You just go to their website and download the app on your phone and computer and subscribe to a monthly or yearly plan. But you may not need this because some newer smartphones now come with free VPNs built in.

THE EMERGENCY STUFF

Here are some basic safety precautions you should take before you hit the road:

- Take photos of your passport, driver's license, and Covid vaccination card and store them on your phone in an album labeled "Important." Now you know where to find them. Then, email a copy to yourself just in case you lose your phone. Finally, print a copy of each and carry them with you!

- If you have an old, spare but still functional phone lying around, it's not a crazy idea to pack it if you're going backpacking. If your primary phone gets stolen or gets water damage, you've got a backup phone. Just backup your photos and videos because those are irreplaceable.

HOMESICKNESS INSURANCE

No matter how thick-skinned and savvy a traveler you are, there will come a time during your trip when you are down in the dumps. To safeguard against a total meltdown when that happens, put the following proactive safeguards in place now. I call them homesickness insurance — the only insurance policy in life that you get to design yourself and enroll in without spending a penny. You're welcome.

Elect Your Support Staff

When you're battling homesickness, nothing does more to soothe the soul than talking to your besties back home. Here's how to line up the perfect on-call team to respond to your SOS.

► *Emotional-Support Humans*

Judiciously choose which family members and friends will be your emotional-support humans while you travel. Let them know that eventually a day will come when you reach out tired, sad, frustrated, and missing them so badly it hurts. Prepare them to understand that this is normal and inevitable. Help them get in the mindset that homesickness is real but not always rational. Because the last thing you need is people prematurely encouraging you to come home when really what you need is an ear to listen or a pep talk.

► *Devil's Advocate*

Your devil's advocate is your trusted voice of reason, while your emotional-support human is your cheerleader. Your emotional-support human is going to tell you, "Everything is going to be okay," whereas your devil's advocate is going to say, "Let's weigh the pros and cons." This person is levelheaded and slow to emotion and is going to assess your situation as best they can and help you come to the logical conclusion of whether it's truly time to stay or go. If your devil's advocate and your emotional-support human are the same person, be clear on what you need from them in the moment: an ear to listen or problem-solving.

Assemble Your Squad

Make a list of four friends and family members who will act as your support system and who you'll keep on speed dial. Which are your comfort people, and which are your devil's advocates?

Once you've decided who you'd like to elect to these positions, call them and let them know they might be hearing from you when times get rough. Promise to return the favor for them someday.

Gather Homesick Letters

Homesick letters are loving notes from your greatest fans back home that you travel with and break out during your low moments. Letters are thin and light, easy to carry, and having this stockpile of encouragement will provide comfort during the hardest times!

So now, before you go, reach out to your favorite humans and ask them if they would be so kind as to pen a few words for you to take with you. Maybe this will even be a fun throwback for them — since who writes actual letters anymore?! If you'll be traveling over your birthday, you can also ask for advance birthday cards. To sweeten the pot for these people, you could write similar letters to them before you go. Even though they'll be staying home, chances are they'll appreciate having a fun reminder of your love for them when they're holding down the fort and missing you.

...And now you're officially prepped!

CHAPTER 15

The Purge

When I left the States on my first one-way ticket, I was young. I was a single, childless, houseless human! I didn't have a career, a cat, or even a car, so my escape was easy! And hello, this is another reason why I want to encourage my little sisters to travel before you make big purchases and big decisions that will limit your freedom!

But let's say you already have the career, the couch, the divorce in process, and/or the house. How do you leave without leaving a total mess behind and disappointing everyone? Well, first, life is messy. Let it be messy! We're going to try our best to make a smooth escape without breaking too many hearts or contracts...but if broken contracts are what it takes, then screw "smooth." Do what you have to do to save your life.

Since I've never sold a house or used a house sitter to watch my cat, I interviewed dozens of men and women who have done just that in order to pursue living life abroad. I expected to hear stressful stories of how hard it was to detach and leave, but nearly everyone I interviewed — from the Brits to the Mexicans — told me that the purge was easy. Almost too easy! Many travelers reported that once they decided to go, the process of leaving happened faster than they had expected. Houses sold quickly, jobs transitioned quickly, subletters moved in quickly — consequently, they began traveling more quickly than anticipated.

The truth is that the hardest part won't be leaving; the hardest part will be making the decision to let go. To trust that the Universe has your back and you're making the right move. PS. That's another book to add to your travel book list: *The Universe Has Your Back* by Gabrielle Bernstein. Total game changer.

However, before we dive in, I realize that not everyone has the same ties to cut. Some people have pets, and some people don't. Some people have heirloom armchairs to store, some people don't. So read whichever parts of this chapter apply to you, and skip the parts that don't.

A little preview of what we're going to cover:

- What to do with your stuff
- Jobs and bosses
- Houses and leases
- Safe havens for your pets and plants
- More things that sound stressful but aren't

So the big question for people with tangible assets and obligations: How do you leave these things permanently or temporarily? Let's discuss what to do with...

THE STUFF

From this day forward, remember that everything you buy is something you are going to have to store or sell or donate when it's time for you to travel. Every time you go to buy a lamp or high heels, ask yourself where you're going to store it when you're *tra-la-la-ing* around South America. Ask yourself, *Does this thing contribute to my trip?* and if it doesn't, don't buy it.

✈ **TRAVEL LESSON #15** ·····································

The less stuff you have, the more free you are.

··

Once you start seeing your stuff as an anchor weighing you down, you won't want it. You'll feel allergic to it.

Now, here's what to do with your stuff before you go.

Store It

Storage costs money. If you have the budget, you can get a storage unit, sure. Google "Storage unit near me" and compare prices. What you pay will depend on how much space you need. See if the storage company offers yearly prices rather than monthly prices. For me, however, paying $150 a month to store my shoe and coat collection didn't make sense. That $150 could be spent on an entire week of accommodations by the beach in Hoi An. So instead, I asked around to see which of my friends could use an extra $50 a month in exchange for storing my things in the corner of their garage or in the back of their basement. After all, I would rather pay my friends than a storage company. If you have parents who love you and have some extra space, your solution is simple: dump your stuff at their house for free.

Sell It

Before I moved to Bulgaria to join the Peace Corps, I took my whole wardrobe to a secondhand store and made a decent profit from clothing I was just going to give away otherwise. Consider selling your things on eBay, Facebook Marketplace, and OfferUp.

▶ *Travel Hack: Have a Going Away Garage Sale Party*

Right before it's time to leave, throw a party (potluck and BYOB) and let your friends know that you'll have items for sale by donation. A friend of mine did this. All her things were for sale by donation, except for a few special treasures that she priced. She made about $2,000 in extra travel cash. The more people drank, the more they bought. Now her friends have trinkets that remind them of her, she has extra travel money, and she got to say a tipsy goodbye to the people she loves.

Donate It

Some collections are meant to be shared, even wine collections! Rather than having your things sit in storage as a reminder of your old life, give. Donate to friends, charities, Goodwill, or NGOs. Let someone else start a new chapter with your old chapter — so you get to move on and write your next chapter (with new things and fewer things this time). Congrats, you're free.

THE JOB

I once had an assistant who broke my heart. I absolutely adored her, and planned the next thirty years of my life with her in the equation, so the day she suddenly came to me and declared that she was leaving to pursue her dream of becoming a chef, I was devastated. In her absence, however, I was forced to pivot and came up with an even better system that I wouldn't have discovered if she hadn't left. Her leaving turned out to be a gift! So consider your leaving part of the divine plan.

When it comes to the job dilemma, the four most common solutions are to:

- quit your job.
- pause your job.
- find a job abroad.
- take your job with you.

If you're quitting, depending on your resources, you can either:

- travel to strategize your next plan of action, then quit.
- quit and then travel to help you decide what to do next.

I have done both with equal potency. Whenever it comes time for you to work again but you're not up for a full-time job back home, you've got chapter 2, "Pick Your Travel Path," to guide the way.

If you are blessed to work for an employer who understands your need to soul-search and feel alive, seek a sabbatical. In many cases, employers would rather give valued employees a pause than lose them altogether. If you're hesitant to ask because you predict they'll say no, don't worry — you have nothing to lose!

When I'm dreaming big — let's say I'm asking Netflix to give me my own travel TV show — and I think it's a long shot, I have more fun with the art of asking, since I'm no longer fixated on the outcome of the question. In fact, one of the mantras that keeps me aiming for the stars is this: "If you don't ask, they can't say yes." At least give them the chance to surprise you! Life is short. Ask the question. Dream big. Believe in miracles. Let the Universe intervene. And if you get a "no," then who cares? You'll find another way to reach your goals.

HOUSES AND LEASES

A woman I play pickleball with lives half-time in Seattle and half-time in Baja Sur. She has kept her condo in Seattle, rents it out to travel nurses on thirteen-week contracts, and makes $5,000 a month in income. These nurses have housing stipends and fixed start and end dates, and if you trust them with your veins, you can trust them with your house!

This is to say that you don't have to sell your condo or house. You can find long-term renters or put it on Airbnb for short-term rentals and hire an agency to handle the logistics. Or...you can sell it.

Renting? Lease isn't over for a while? Here are some steps you can take if you want to get out of your lease:

1. **Review your lease agreement:** Your lease agreement may include a provision about early termination. Read the agreement carefully to see if there are any options for breaking the lease and what the penalties may be.

2. **Discuss the situation with your landlord:** Talk to your landlord about your situation and explain why you need to break the lease. Your landlord may be willing to work with you to find a solution, such as finding a replacement tenant or negotiating a lease termination agreement.

3. **Understand the consequences:** Breaking a lease can have consequences, such as losing your security deposit and being responsible for rent until a new tenant is found. Be sure to weigh the risks before making a decision. If you're renting, consider this: How much is your cost of living where you are now vs. the cost of living of where you want to go next? Can you save

money by moving? Then maybe losing that security deposit is worth it.

Listen, I am not the expert on real estate, but a quick You-Tube search will lead you toward thousands of nomads who have gone through the process of buying or building a home abroad and are full of wisdom and resources.

PETS AND PLANTS

Do you take your dog traveling, or do you leave it at home? The answer totally depends on where you're going.

Thinking of taking your dog to Bali? Don't do it. Not only is it technically illegal to import an animal into Indonesia, but it's also dangerous for your pet. Animal rights aren't really a thing in Bali. Barking dogs are often poisoned, there aren't any safe places for your animal to roam free, and the population of Bali street dogs will kick you LA dog's ass.

Conversely, visit Puerto Vallarta, and you'll find plenty of snowbirds living their best lives under the sun with their dogs and cats, which they brought from Canada or the US. Import laws are more relaxed in Mexico, travel time isn't too stressful for the animal if you're coming from North America, and taking your dog for a walk on a leash down the Malecón is a joy.

So, before you plan a move with your pet, you need to know if it's feasible, affordable, and safe. You need to know the regulations and laws about bringing a pet. Google "traveling with pets" + your destination. You can also search for "best pet shipping companies," and you'll find pet travel agencies that can answer your questions and even assist you with the move. For example, recently PetAir UK helped a friend of mine bring his dog from the UK to Thailand. They handled all the paperwork and transportation for a flat fee, and now that dog has a bar named after him in Chiang Mai: The George.

After you've done your research, take your remaining questions to travel-specific or destination-specific expat Facebook groups to find travelers with pets who can offer first-hand experiences, recommendations, and advice.

Pets are family. Leaving them behind doesn't always feel right, but sometimes it makes sense for the pet to stay in their familiar space, especially when you plan to be moving from location to location. Consider long-term boarding, asking a friend to watch your pet, or hiring a pet sitter.

Oh and what about plants? I once was a house sitter for a couple with a garden, no pets. They had a beautiful yard that needed to be maintained while they were away, so they hired me. No yard, just houseplants? Move them to a friend's house, but do take responsibility for finding them the ideal sunlight locations, and teach your friend how to handle a dying plant. Save us all the stress!

FAMILY AND FRIENDS

Before I left for the Peace Corps, a super religious friend called me and told me that Jesus came to her in a dream and told her I was going to die in Bulgaria. I'm all for communication with God or the Universe, but this didn't feel like God or the Universe — this felt like a projection of fear.

You need to decipher between when someone has a valid point and when someone is just projecting their fear onto you. Be smart and do research on where you're going and make sure that you're not casually walking into a war zone without a plan. Safety, crime, and health should all be factors you weigh when choosing a destination, but your old Aunt Kathy who still thinks Yugoslavia is a country should not be allowed to influence whether you stay or go. Do not let other people's fear dictate your decisions.

A DISCOVERY MISSION

If you've read this whole chapter and are still hesitant about selling your apartment and quitting your job, then don't.

Don't quit your job. Don't give away your apartment. Don't burn your whole life to the ground. Tell your clients that you're going to go find inspiration and you'll be back. Leave your dog with a friend. And go travel! Go for a few weeks or a few months. Go with the questions and see if you can find the answers. I call this travel approach going on a Discovery Mission.

A Discovery Mission is a low-commitment exploration to find out what's missing in your life without setting your entire life on fire. Your Discovery Mission is centered around asking these questions:

- Where and how do I find work? Or how long can I travel with the savings I've budgeted?
- Which city excites me?
- Where can I afford to move now?
- Where do I already have friends or feel like I could make friends?
- Can I bring my dog or cat?

That's it. Go with the questions and see if you can find the answers. If you find the answers and find the place, then you can make the moves to move. If you don't find the answers, don't give up on the questions. Go home, plan a new trip next year, and try again — but don't sit and wonder *how?* for fifteen years. Go figure it out! If you never go, you'll never know!

CHAPTER 16

Leaving and Landing

Can I tell you a secret? I'm afraid of flying! Especially long flights over the ocean. And I know I'm not the only one! I get messages all the time from women on the verge of a panic attack, thinking about canceling their flight.

But you know, since it's literally my job to fly around the world, I've figured out how to hack my own panic attacks related to both flying and landing in a new country — and I want to share them with you, starting with...

✈ **TRAVEL LESSON #16** ·································

Plan the first five hours of your trip.

··

Anxiety comes from not having control or not knowing what to expect, so have every detail of the first five hours of your trip planned, starting from the moment you land.

THE FIRST-FIVE-HOURS PLAN CHECKLIST

Know...
- ❏ Your visa and immigration requirements
- ❏ Address of where you're staying

❏   Whether you need proof of onward travel

❏   How much local currency you'll get at the airport ATM

❏   Whether the airport has wifi and/or whether you need to buy a SIM card when you land

❏   How you're getting to your hotel (prearranged driver, taxi, airport shuttle to the city, rideshare, etc.)

❏   If your hotel's reception desk will be open or you need a code to get into your Airbnb

❏   What you'll have as your first meal (do you need to grab airport snacks or are there restaurants open nearby?)

❏   How to navigate to your destination. (Will you use maps offline or will you have internet to navigate?)

Pro tip: Before you fly, do a YouTube search of your destination airport, and get a visual tutorial of what to expect.

Now you don't have to think about what happens when you land. Future you has got it covered. Instead of being thrown into the unknown, you know exactly what to do when you land. For me, this dissolves my anxiety by giving me a to-do list to focus on.

THE DAY BEFORE YOUR FLIGHT

Here are my rules, habits, and advice to make your travel day as zen as can be.

♦   Check in online: If you have booked directly with the airline, you can usually check in online twenty-four hours before a flight. If a passport is not required, you can print your boarding pass and head straight to security. If a passport check is required, still check in online to confirm your seat. (When you arrive at the airport, check to see if the airline offers an expedited line or a "bag drop" line for people who have already checked in online.)

◆ Have your passport, wallet, and outfit ready.

◆ Have your bags packed. I make sure my under-the-seat carry-on has these essentials:

o   hand sanitizer

o   wet wipes

o   snacks (nuts, energy bars, crackers)

o   face mist and/or moisturizer

o   toothbrush and toothpaste

o   face mask (the Covid kind and the skincare kind — yes, I'm that girl wearing a sheet mask on the flight)

o   Tylenol and/or Tylenol PM

o   a shawl to adapt to changing temperatures

o   charging cables

o   earbuds or headphones

o   fully charged electronics with downloaded audiobooks and movies

o   a book

o   always a pen and journal

o   extra articles of clothing, if needed: a fresh outfit to put on if I'm meeting someone special or extra layers if I'm landing in a different climate

◆ Know how you're getting to the airport.

◆ If you've got an early flight, give yourself enough time to wake up, shower, and ease into the day. Do what you'd normally do, just earlier because the worst feeling in the world is scrambling to get to the airport.

◆ Instead of constantly checking your phone, paranoid that you're going to be late, set an alarm for thirty minutes before you need to leave for the airport, and relax until then.

- ◆ Do not drink too much the day before your flight. Hangovers + airports + flights = anxiety.

- ◆ Pack a reusable water bottle (I prefer the ones that collapse to save space) in your carry-on to fill up at a water fountain after you go through security.

- ◆ Know which lounge you want to hit up and build in enough time to grab a quick bite and a mimosa before your flight.

Now it's time to go to the airport. Let me hold your hand through this one, too.

ON TRAVEL DAY

I know that if I rush the process of going to the airport, I will have a panic attack. Therefore, I treat myself extra gently. I wake up and stretch while telling myself positive mantras like *I am so grateful that I get to go to Cambodia today.* I give myself time for a long bath or shower. I catch myself when I'm rushing and slow myself down with deep breaths.

If my anxiety is really bad, I ask myself one question: *Would you rather not go?* 'Cause that's the option. Go or don't. Then a voice inside me screams, *Oh, I'm going!* Now I'm determined to get on that plane. My determination overshadows my doubts. And then I distract myself with travel treats: I give myself things to look forward to at the airport, whether it's a 7 AM glass of wine in the lounge or McDonald's (I'm so American, I know).

When I'm at the airport and those treats don't calm me down, I recite the facts: Flying is the safest form of transport ever. Aircrafts are built to handle turbulence, storms, and even being struck by lightning. Also, flight attendants aren't scared to fly. If they aren't scared, you don't need to be scared.

I give myself things to be excited for on the flight, like an audiobook or a movie about my destination. If it's a flight longer than seven hours, I knock myself out with a Tylenol PM and just look forward to a long sleep. And no, I don't bring my own airplane pillow. I just use the pillows they provide on the plane.

Now that you're in your seat, let the pros do the work. Your job is simply to sit and do nothing besides stay hydrated (low humidity levels in the cabin can dehydrate you). Keep your eyes on the prize. Keep thinking about why you're doing this, where you're going, and all the amazing things waiting for you!

Smooth Landing

Depending on the destination, as you're about to land, the flight attendants may give you a couple forms to fill out.

◆ **Immigration form:** This asks for your basic info and the address of where you're staying (just write the name of the first hotel or the address of your host's place).

◆ **Declarations form:** They want to know if you're bringing live animals, produce, or over $10,000 in cash. Usually the answer is no ... as long as you're not carrying a sandwich. Don't be like the girl who got fined $1,844 USD for bringing a Subway sandwich into Australia. True story.

Tinkle on the plane before the seatbelt sign is turned on so that you can head straight to the front of the Immigration line when you disembark. Meeting someone special? Change your clothes, brush your teeth, and use those baby wipes to give yourself a mini-makeover on the plane so you make it through Immigration quickly. When you land at your final destination, don't dillydally!

What to say to Immigration as a tourist: Whenever you're entering a country on a tourist visa and Immigration asks you why you're coming into the country, tell them you're coming for vacation. Even if you plan to work on your laptop and rent a villa or look into setting up a business, you are currently only allowed to be a tourist. Don't get fancy here.

After Immigration, you'll collect your bags, go through Customs, and officially enter the arrival hall and the country! The arrival hall is where you'll find ATMs, SIM card stands, taxi/bus stands, and your driver if they are waiting for you!

PS. Need help in the airport? Almost always, there is a general information desk with someone that speaks English. Their only job is to help you.

You've got your five-hour plan in place, so now you can breeze right through to your hotel!

GETTING OUT OF THE AIRPORT — AND GETTING SETTLED

Once you leave the airport and get to your lodging, it all might hit you.

New sounds. New smells. New beds. There's always an adjustment period.

Soon after landing in Bulgaria for the first time, I was driven to a small village in the mountains, where my host family greeted me on a dirt road and whisked me inside to feed me something I didn't recognize. At first, I thought it was a bull testicle. Then I thought it was a meatball. Then I was startled to find a gooey egg inside! I couldn't figure out what the hell I was eating (I had never seen a Scotch egg before).

I was so nervous that I held the knife by the sharp part and tried to cut my food with the handle while my new *baba* watched with concern. I was so out of my element that I felt like a newborn baby. I didn't know how to use the shower, the front door, or my hands!

This will happen. Sometimes, when you land, you get overwhelmed. That's normal and almost expected. So how do you work through it?

Five Ways to Settle Softly

1. **Drink water.** After a long flight or bus ride, your body needs hydration. Water is actually a natural antianxiety elixir.

2. **Take a shower.** There's no better feeling than taking a shower and changing your undies after a long flight! Just don't get naked until you've figured out how to get the shower to turn on and the hot water to come out.

3. **Stimulate your senses with something familiar.** A coke, a banana, M&Ms. Although I must tell you, all these things might taste slightly different abroad, especially bananas!

4. **Don't hide in your room.** Go to the social area, go for a walk around the block, or go to the local convenience store and introduce yourself to the snacks. Get out of your room and meet the world.

5. **See where you are.** I like to pull up Google Maps when I arrive at my location and just see what pops up around me. Use the search bar to find massages and coffee! Read the reviews. Give yourself your first

mission. The first day is for getting oriented. Don't try to push yourself to have a full schedule. Wake up slowly, go to breakfast, and then wander.

How to Acclimate

After that initial settling-in session, you have two more things to do.

▶ First, Do Everything You Can to Avoid Jet Lag

Have you ever felt like you're in a fog after a long flight? That's jet lag. Jet lag is when you travel across different time zones, and your internal body clock is out of sync with the new time zone, making you feel like you just woke up from a nap in the middle of the night or like you're ready for bed at lunchtime.

But don't worry! There are ways to combat jet lag:

1. **Hydrate.** Dehydration makes jet lag worse, so drink plenty of water and electrolytes.
2. **Get on a normal time schedule ASAP.** No matter what time you've landed, you are only allowed to sleep between 9 PM and 8 AM. If you do not get this right on day one, you will be screwed for the next five days. Stay up 'til 9 PM. Drink a coke, a coffee, or whatever you need to make sure you don't fall asleep too early.
3. **Take melatonin.** Can't sleep? Melatonin is my secret weapon for getting on a normal sleep cycle and can help reset your body clock.
4. **Get some sunlight.** Exposure to natural light can help reset your body clock. Try to spend some time outdoors during daylight hours, especially in the morning.

5. **Take naps.** Short naps, around twenty to thirty minutes, can help you stay alert and fight fatigue.

▶ *Next, Decide Who You're Going to Be*

Set your intentions for the day. Are you going to be the girl who says yes? The girl who talks to strangers? The girl who goes for a run in the morning? Create the girl you want to release into the world. Mindset is everything. *Everyyyyyything!* Because guess what? In an unfamiliar place, your instinct may be to protect yourself and stay closed. Instead, see this unfamiliar place as your blank slate, and remain open to new possibilities. Away from friends, family, bosses, and routines — you're given a chance to redefine everything you have ever wanted out of life.

Journal Challenge

If you're serious about using this trip as a catalyst for growth and self-discovery, join my 21-Day One-Way Magic Journal Challenge.

They say it takes twenty-one days to develop a habit that sticks, so let's do it together. You can join the challenge before your trip or during your trip to start bridging the gap between who you are now and who you want to be. Thoughtful daydreaming is the key to unlocking the magic within you, and I'm going to guide you through that journey. Begin the challenge at Alexa-West.com/OneWay.

PART FOUR

STAYING AND GOING

CHAPTER 17

Staying a While

Get ready for a love story.

One summer, I jumped in my bestie's car, and we took a road trip around Baja Sur, Mexico, to research and write our Baja Sur travel guidebook. During that trip, Emilia met and fell in love with a Spanish guy who was introduced to her by a mutual friend from Spain. After spending just one week together, Emilia knew that she wanted to fly to Spain and spend more time with him. And she did. And it went really, *really* well. After a year of flying back and forth between Spain and Mexico, Emilia and Enrique decided to make it official... in the Spanish way!

In Spain, couples who are not married can register to become legal domestic partners, known as *pareja de hecho*. After a year of living with Enrique, my little Mexican traveler is in love and has been granted her Spanish residency, which, by the way, includes health insurance. She's really excited about health insurance. In one year or two, she'll be able to apply for citizenship and get her Spanish passport. What a dream come true!

I'm not suggesting that you hunt down a Spanish guy and make him fall in love with you just so you can get a Spanish passport (however, if you do, please write a book about it because I'd totally read that), but certainly don't count out the possibility of falling in love and moving to another country. And certainly don't limit yourself to thinking that you have to grow in the country you were born in. You can grow anywhere. You were planted on Earth, and Earth is your home. Borders are just imaginary lines we've drawn on a map.

✈ TRAVEL LESSON #17 ·······················

You can live anywhere you want.

···

It's not uncommon for travelers to find themselves living abroad by accident, and you may be no exception. Maybe you intend to go on a one-month trip to Kenya, but five years later, you're still there, running women's retreats at a wildlife conservation center. This kind of thing happens all the time. Want proof? The next time you travel and meet expats abroad, ask them how they ended up living in Nicaragua (or wherever) for ten years, and they'll likely tell you it was a happy accident.

I want you to dream big. Screw "being realistic." But I also want you to understand the framework and foundation of what it takes to be an expat — aka a traveler who lives outside their home country for an extended period. Whether you intentionally set out to find a new home or you accidentally settle down for a bit, let me save you time and stress by fast-tracking you to the front of the "move abroad" line.

HOW DO YOU MOVE ABROAD?

First, what do I mean by "move"?

Moving abroad isn't like moving from Alaska to Texas (although that might feel like you've moved to another planet).

You're not taking your bed or kitchen utensils with you when you move abroad. Instead, there are major rules to follow and adjustments to make in order for you to move to another country. Let's discuss.

Your ability to move will heavily rely on these six things:

1. Work and money
2. Visas
3. Taxes
4. Housing
5. Healthcare
6. Happiness

In this chapter, we'll cover it all, but before I give you the keys to the castle, I need you to understand how much of an impact your move is going to have on whichever place you choose.

YOUR IMPACT

Digital nomadism is a global phenomenon that shows no signs of slowing down. The number of American digital nomads more than doubled in recent years — from 4.8 million in 2018 to 10.9 million in 2020. And while that number seems impressive now, the common projection is that the estimated number of digital nomads worldwide could reach 1 billion by 2035.

So how do we spread out around the world without totally destroying it? How do we go searching for paradise without erasing the essence of the places we go? The answer: We can't, really. The presence of tourism changes things. Period.

Some changes are good. Tourism tends to bring new jobs and stimulate the economy. Some changes are bad. The influx of remote workers and nomads can negatively impact delicate communities. The increased demand for housing and other resources eventually leads to inflation, making it nearly impossible for locals to afford rent, land, or basic necessities. This imbalance can lead to a rise in poverty, then crime, and eventually a tense divide between foreigners and locals.

Anywhere you travel, you must bring a balance. You can't just take. You need to give. You can't just consume. You need to contribute.

It's time for us to know better and to do better, especially as long-term travelers and expats. For us to move forward with this nomad movement without destroying communities or the planet, we've got to be the captains of our own ships and not throw all our metaphorical (and literal) trash and baggage overboard.

So, when you travel, how will you give back? Or how will you make sure that you're not taking more than you're giving?

Start with this: Support eco-tourism, local shops, and small businesses. Be a good person, have respect, show interest in the culture, and vote with your dollar. That's a great start.

And if you plan to stay longer as an expat or a digital nomad, here are some specific things you can do:

◆ Learn the language so that you can participate in the community.

◆ Study the culture and traditions so that you can respect and preserve them.

◆ Organize beach cleanups and language exchanges.

◆ Always show gratitude that you are allowed to spend time in a place that you love.

◆ Take inspiration from expats around the world who are leading initiatives such as foreign-funded animal shelters in Bali or wildlife conservation projects in Costa Rica.

As you travel the world, look for opportunities to give back and leave a place better than you found it.

THE PRACTICAL LAYERS
OF LIVING ABROAD

Now that you know better, let's explore the layers of living abroad.

Layer 1: Work and Money

What can you and can't you legally do to make an income in a country that's not your own?

I run Facebook communities for women traveling the world. They are so supportive, and we learn a lot from each other's experiences. I love all these girls … except for one.

One morning, I received a message from a girl from Morocco that really pissed me off. It read, "I've just arrived in Bali looking for work. I'm broke and I have no money to pay rent or buy food. I need to start tattooing in Bali immediately so I can afford to live here. Can you please allow me to advertise my services? I'm so broke."

I took a deep, triggered breath and replied, "I am so sorry that you're in this position. Unfortunately, without the proper visa, it's illegal for you to work here. When you have the proper visa, I'd be delighted to help."

What I really wanted to say was, "Um, hello! What were you thinking coming here with no money and no way to legally support yourself? Also, are you really trying to take jobs away from local tattoo artists? Please know better and do better." *Clearly, she needed this book!*

You can't just land in a country and work without permission. It doesn't work like that. In fact your job as a tourist is to spend money, not make money. It's your job to give to the local economy, not take from it. So if you want to make money in a foreign country, plan ahead.

In chapter 2, we broke down a plethora of ways to work abroad, both online and for a foreign company. So let's quickly review the two main ways to make money while traveling:

1. Work online as a digital nomad, where your money comes from outside your destination/host country.
2. Find a job in the host country that will sponsor your visa and let you work there legally.

Anything else, if you are taking money from the local economy without a work permit or the proper visa, would be considered illegal.

That being said, I have friends who work as Botox queens in Mexico, hairdressers in Bali, and tennis coaches in Dubai. They are either hired by a local company or start their own businesses. It's possible to make it happen. Revisit chapter 2 and see how I recommend you do this, but also, let's talk about the visas that bring these long-term travel dreams to life.

Layer 2: Visas

How do you legally reside in another country long-term? You can't just show up and stay for as long as you want or get a job right away. You need the proper visa.

You already know about tourist visas. Tourist visas are for vacation purposes and short-term stays only. Do not plan to make money in that country as a tourist. If you work from your laptop, do so discreetly and make sure your money comes from outside that country. Otherwise, you're taking money away from locals, and that's illegal without the proper visa.

Want to stay longer than a tourist? Here are some visas to search for around the world and a few stipulations they come with:

- **Work visa:** This visa will almost always be sponsored by a company that has hired you, and it allows you to make money in the country in local currency.
- **Business visa:** This isn't the same as a work visa, but it will usually allow you to hold meetings and do research.
- **Education or student visa:** Study a language or a craft.
- **Investor visa:** You must invest in land, property, or a business or agree to keep a hefty lump sum in a bank account in that country. These visas don't offer citizenship.
- **Golden visa:** Also known as "citizenship by investment" or "residency by investment," these programs are offered by a number of countries around the world. They allow foreign nationals to obtain residency or citizenship in a country by making a large investment.
- **Retirement visa:** If you meet certain age and financial requirements, you can stay long-term.
- **Digital nomad visa:** These visas are becoming more common as digital nomadism becomes more common. Here is an example of how they work: As of 2023, Portugal offers a temporary residence permit for remote workers, also known as the "D7 visa." This visa allows digital nomads to live and work in Portugal for up to one year, with the option to renew for another two years, as long as they can prove that their remote

job pays at least 2,800 EUR (roughly $3,100 USD) a month — along with a few other stipulations — including proof of housing and insurance. Nomads pay 15 percent income tax in Portugal, and now Portugal gets more tax revenue in addition to more economic stimulation.

As for permanent residency, some countries will allow you to apply for residency and/or citizenship, usually if you invest a certain amount of money or marry a citizen.

▶ *How Do You Get These Visas?*

Check out CIBTvisas.com, where you can find a list of visa options for your destination. When you select a visa, click "view requirements" to see if you meet them.

I know this all may sound a little overwhelming, especially because every country offers different visas with different stipulations. The good news is that you don't have to go through these visa processes alone. In almost every country, you'll find visa agencies that help foreigners legally obtain visas that suit their needs. For a fee, of course.

In short, the most common approaches to legally moving to a foreign country are obtaining one of the following:

♦ **A visa** that allows you to stay longer than a tourist visa — like a student visa, digital nomad visa, business visa, or retirement visa.

♦ **Residency**, which grants you certain residential privileges like opening a bank account, running a business, or accessing public health coverage.

♦ **Citizenship**, which grants you a passport.

My Visa Advice

Slow down. Start with a tourist visa, figure out if you click with a place, and if you do, extend to longer visas and then consider more permanent steps.

Oh, and you're going to get tired of tourist visas eventually. Moving to a new country every thirty to sixty days gets exhausting quickly. So let your visa allowance guide your travels. Longer visa allowances mean less moving; less moving means less spending; and less spending means traveling longer.

Know your visa options before you start dreaming up a big impossible plan!

Layer 3: Taxes

Who's taking your money?

First, let me tell you that I'm not a tax specialist or a CPA. Triple-check all this information as it applies to you before you plan your whole life around what I'm about to tell you.

Now, I've got bad news for Americans and great news for everyone else ...

The United States of America is the only country in the world (besides North Korea) that follows a citizenship-based tax system, meaning that citizens are required to pay taxes on their worldwide income regardless of where they live.

The rest of the world follows "territorial taxation," where only income or profits earned within the geographic borders of a country are subject to taxation by that country's government. In other words, in territorial taxation, the tax system only applies to activities and transactions that take place within the country's territorial boundaries, regardless of the nationality or residence status of the taxpayer.

Under territorial taxation, income earned outside the country is generally not subject to taxation in that country, even if the taxpayer is a resident or citizen of that country. This means that individuals and businesses can potentially reduce their tax liabilities by generating income outside their home country.

The general rule is that taxes are for residents, not necessarily citizens…unless you're from the US. According to the IRS, "If you are a US citizen or a resident alien living outside the United States, your worldwide income is subject to US income tax, regardless of where you live."

Let's say you're living in South Korea for an entire year, make your money outside the US, and never set foot in the US that year. You still must file a tax return in the US and potentially pay taxes — even if you are taxed in South Korea. However, the US has tax treaties with many countries, including South Korea, to prevent double taxation on the same income. These treaties typically provide rules to allocate taxing rights between the two countries and to provide relief from double taxation.

In short: Americans file a tax return and potentially pay taxes forever no matter where they live. Everyone else, be grateful.

There is some exciting tax news for American expats, however. If you live outside the US for more than 330 days within a twelve-month period (it doesn't matter whether it's from April to April or November to November — just within a twelve-month period), you may qualify for the Foreign Earned Income Exclusion (FEIE), which allows you to exclude a certain amount of your foreign earned income from US federal income tax. The exclusion amount is adjusted for inflation each year, and for the 2023 tax year, the maximum exclusion amount is $120,000 USD. However, it's important to note that the FEIE is not a deduction, it is an exclusion — which means that the qualifying income is not included in your taxable income. It's also important to note that the FEIE is not automatic and must be claimed on your tax return.

But then it gets complicated again because if you're an American with over $10,000 USD in a foreign bank account, you are required to file the FBAR (Report of Foreign Bank and Financial Accounts) because, like a psycho boyfriend, the IRS feels like they have a right to know how you make and spend your money. This requirement is part of the US government's efforts to combat tax evasion and money laundering.

If you're doing business abroad, you need an accountant who knows how to handle digital nomad and expat taxes!

Layer 4: Housing

I've lived in private pool villas in Bali, ocean-view condos in Mexico, and high-rise apartment buildings smack-dab in the middle of Bangkok! In many expat hubs or big cities, you'll easily find plenty of housing listings offering short-term and long-term leases.

Two bonuses to renting in tourist areas or big cities abroad:

◆ Apartments and houses are usually furnished.
◆ Short-term rentals are common, typically starting at a minimum of a one-month commitment.

▶ *How Do You Find These Places?*

1. **Facebook groups:** Look for rental or housing groups in your destination, and you'll find rooms or houses listed by subletters, owners, or agencies.
2. **Rental agencies:** In big cities like Taipei, you can contact an agency and tell them your exact specifications

(two-bedroom apartment with a desk within a certain neighborhood and budget), and they'll find a place for you, for a fee paid by either you or the property owner. Find the most trusted agencies in expat Facebook groups, where you can get firsthand recommendations.

3. **Guesthouses or hotels:** I live in guesthouses and hotels all the time! I love having built-in security, breakfasts, housekeepers, and utilities included. Show up, walk around, and keep an eye out for a place you might want to stay. Making a deal face-to-face is usually better than the deals offered online.

4. **Airbnb:** Go on Airbnb and use the "month" and "week" features to find houses at a discounted price. Read the reviews and look for clues about the location! Location is everything.

   Note about Airbnb: The crazy development of Airbnb is one of the biggest causes of gentrification for some local economies around the world where housing is becoming unaffordable for locals. I believe a solution is coming so that we won't have to boycott Airbnb forever (Portugal and Bangkok have started enforcing Airbnb regulations), but for now, keep this in mind while you shop around and perhaps consider other options when possible.

▶ *Pro Housing Tip: Go See the Property before You Rent*

Now, I know you are excited and want to have a house or a villa waiting for you when you land, but I have one big piece of advice: either go see the house before you rent it or make sure the place you're renting has fabulous reviews on Google or Airbnb so that you can confirm it's not a scam.

Here's what I mean: I had a girlfriend who wanted to live in Bali. She told me she found a dreamy house and was about to put down a six-month deposit, sight unseen, while she was back in the Netherlands. (A six-month deposit sounds crazy but is not totally uncommon in Bali.) Me, having learned my lesson far too many times, insisted that I go see it before she paid. Thank goodness I did! When I arrived at the villa, it looked nothing like the photos. The kitchen was full of mold, and the wifi was so slow it was unusable. (Always test the wifi when viewing a villa or a house. Just google "wifi speed test," and you'll find a speed tester to run.) She didn't end up renting it.

Before you book a place, investigate these factors:

- Is the location good or walkable?
- Will you need a bike or a car?
- Is it close to public transport?
- Are there restaurants or markets nearby?
- What about the noise? Is it close to a main road where loud motorbikes buzz by nonstop?
- Does it smell weird?
- Do you feel safe?
- How's the wifi?
- Are utilities included?
- Is there air-conditioning? If it's a cooler climate, is there adequate heating?
- Is there reliable hot water?

Make a checklist of what's important to you, visit properties in person, and compare.

Because I'm extra, I made an entire video tutorial on how to find the best houses in Bali. The methods I outline can be applied to many destinations abroad. You can check it out on my YouTube channel.

▶ *What about Buying a House or Land as a Foreigner?*

Take my advice: Don't even think of buying or building for at least the first year of living in a new country. Rent, house-sit, house-swap. If you still want to buy a house or land after you've been there a while, ask yourself these questions:

1. **Can you actually own land as a foreigner?** Imagine if Americans could just walk into Thailand, buy up all the houses, whitewash towns, drive up prices, and kick locals out of their own communities. Kind of like what mainlanders have done to Hawaii. What a nightmare for Thailand, right? So, in many countries, foreigners cannot own land. In Thailand (and most of Asia), foreigners can only buy property if they have a local business partner or friend who owns the majority percentage and the foreigner (that's you) owns a smaller percentage. In Bali, foreigners can lease land from the landowner and build on it, but not own it. I've never understood why you'd want to rent land and build on it knowing that it isn't guaranteed to be yours in twenty years, but whatever. Each country is different, but a quick way to suss out the situation is to talk to a real estate professional or an expat who has been through the processes you're interested in.

2. **By building, are you contributing to or destroying that community?** This is an issue particularly in Bali. Foreigners and locals are buying up land and tearing down tropical landscapes to build villas to either live in or rent out. Housing prices have skyrocketed, and rice fields have disappeared. People will say, "Tourism is ruining the island," but really, lack of regulation is ruining the island. The issue is more about responsible development and environmental

sustainability. I fear that the island will soon be nothing but traffic and empty villas, built at too quick a pace, and soon we will look back and say, "What did we do to Bali?"

So remember this: Just because you can build or buy doesn't mean you should. Rent first and consider the potential impact on the local community and environment before building or buying property.

Layer 5: Healthcare

If you have emergency travel insurance, I'm proud of you. That insurance should cover you in the case of unforeseen accidents or mishaps for the amount of time specified by your policy (say, six months or a year, often with the option of purchasing a new policy once that time is up). But what if you're living abroad or being nomadic and want to pop into the doctor's office for medical care that is not an emergency — for example, if you want to adjust a medication you're on? This visit will not be covered by your travel insurance as it's not an emergency. So how do you see a doctor while living abroad?

Option 1: If you move abroad on a visa that grants you residency or citizenship and that country offers universal healthcare, then you'll likely have access to health insurance. Easy.

Option 2: You can pay out of pocket. Remember I told you that I fly to Puerto Vallarta to get my teeth cleaned? Well, I also get my annual exams and other general medical needs met in Mexico, where I pay out of pocket and it's cheap. I'm talkin' like $50 for a doctor's visit and medication, which is way less than I'd pay in the United States. In fact, paying out of pocket for medical care in countries where it is more affordable is a common strategy for many expats and travelers.

Option 3: You can get expat or nomad insurance. These are insurance plans specifically designed for remote workers and nomadic people who do not have insurance through an employer or the country they're in. Check out your nomad health insurance options at Alexa-West.com/OneWay.

You might find yourself using a mixture of these tactics. Usually when I'm backpacking, I only travel with emergency travel insurance and pay out of pocket when I want to visit a doctor. When my nomad career blessed me with a visa in South Korea while I was teaching, it gave me insurance. When that contract ended, I went back to traveling with just emergency travel insurance. Honestly, in the past, there weren't great nomad insurance options available to me, but now that remote work is becoming more mainstream, we are seeing more affordable and practical insurance options that cater to us travelers. All of these options are worth exploring.

Layer 6: Happiness

Where does your happiness come from on the other side of the world?

I once matched with an Australian guy on Tinder who had a very naive plan. He told me that he was going to move to a small village in Thailand forever. Despite that being logistically impossible for a broke thirty-three-year-old who doesn't work online, I can tell you for certain that village life was not going to be enough for this guy *forever*. His fantasy of being the white savior worshipped by Thai women wasn't going to play out the way he thought it would.

How do I know that I'm absolutely right about this? I've

lived in Thailand long enough to witness with my own eyes the natural progression of foreign men going from hopeful to hateful. Just go to Pattaya or Phuket, and you'll pass tons of "girly bars" where you'll see a bunch of fat white guys sitting at the bar, paying for Thai girls' affection. These girls are clever. They feed these men fried rice, beer, and attention, and the men spend all their money getting beer bods and paying these girls' rent.

I guess these men are contributing to the local economy, so props to them for that at least. But over time, these girly-bar-loving men change. They arrive cheerful and are all "I'm living my best life," but fast-forward a couple years and they usually decay into angry, lonely, unhappy people. Why? Because repetition without purpose is depressing.

To maintain happiness, you must be chasing at least one of three things: purpose, curiosity, or goals. If you are not chasing one of those three things, you are doomed to become an old, bitter expat.

All right, now that I've insulted thousands of men around the world, I can tell you that intentionally seeking your happy place is a worthy cause, and you very well may find it.

I have plenty of friends who have lived in Cambodia for ten-plus years, in Bali for twenty-plus years, or in Mexico for thirty-plus years — and what keeps them there is more than relaxation. It is purpose, it is people, it is something bigger than them. These expats usually have businesses or foundations, or they have married a local and started a family. They have found their happy place because they've found their happy purpose.

Before you go declaring, "I'm going to live here forever," give yourself time to get through the honeymoon phase. When it comes to destinations, date around. Travel around. See what's out there. Be the Travel Bachelorette, and then make your choice.

You're growing at hyperspeed while you travel, which means you might outgrow a place at hyperspeed. Stay open to the idea that "forever" is overrated but "a while" is wonderful. Instead of saying, "I'm going to stay here forever," take the pressure off yourself and off the location. Replace that sentence with "I'm going to stay a while."

We are not Western saviors. We are not saving the day by gracing poorer communities with our presence. But oftentimes, when you're coming from a Western country, you carry privilege. It's how you use your privilege that matters — and in some corners of the world, we can use this privilege to uplift a community rather than destroy it.

I'd like to end this chapter with a shout-out to Portugal. Portugal has approved new laws and regulations to control Airbnb and rental prices because the country is having a major housing crisis. They have also regulated golden visas, which used to allow rich people to essentially buy citizenship. The prime minister has expressed concerns about the impact of tourism on the country's authenticity and has emphasized the need to prioritize the well-being of residents, saying he doesn't want Portugal to become some "sort of Disneyland" and that "there is no city that can remain authentic if it isn't able to maintain its residents." I believe Portugal is the pioneer of welcoming digital nomads while maintaining respect for its people. You go, Portugal!

There's not much more to lecture you on in this chapter, except I will leave you with this: Find your people, and you have found a home. People are home. Oh, and don't work illegally.

CHAPTER 18

Homesick and Going Home

If you travel long enough, you begin to fetishize things you miss from home.

When you're staying in hostel dorms, you miss sleeping naked. When you're eating nothing but rice and noodles, you miss fresh veggies not covered in oil. When you're in a conservative or misogynistic culture, you miss going out in a hot little minidress.

You will miss a lot of things when you're all the way on the other side of the world. You'll miss your niece. You'll miss your skincare routine. You'll miss refrigerated milk, bubble baths, sidewalks, and a postal system you can trust not to lose your stuff. On a rough day, when you're hot and hungry and take the subway in the wrong direction, all you will want to do is teleport home, where life is safe and familiar and contains a fridge full of your favorite things. Then, my dear, you are officially homesick.

Getting homesick because you specifically miss home makes sense. But beware! Sometimes you're homesick because you loathe where you are. Rose-colored glasses truly do wear off, and sometimes they're replaced with shit-colored glasses where everything just sucks.

I remember being halfway through my second teaching

contract in South Korea, in the dead of winter, and feeling so homesick that I was considering doing a "runner" — which is basically leaving the country in the middle of the night and not telling your school that you're leaving. Teachers do this when their teaching jobs are really crappy and they know they'll get penalized for leaving early. Hence the silent escape. My school wasn't bad, though. I loved my boss and my students to death. I just couldn't stand being in South Korea anymore. Hearing "Gangnam Style" everywhere I went, the skin-whitening obsession, and the fact that I don't love Korean food (made worse because *kimbap* looks like sushi but isn't sushi) began to make me unreasonably angry. Also, I had a Canadian coteacher who sat next to me in our tiny teacher's room and would suck on those artificial crab sticks you put in sushi rolls. Yes, suck on them! She also peeled boiled eggs at her desk and would just leave the shells there. It smelled. It was gross. And that's what I had to sit next to every morning.

So, yeah, after one and a half years in South Korea, I was over it. It was a cultural mismatch. A misalignment of what I'd imagined my life to be versus what it became. This made me absolutely cantankerous, which made me want to go home.

At some point, you will hit a wall. You've been traveling so long that your travel fuse is getting shorter and shorter every day, and you can't seem to escape the little micro-annoyances around every corner. Everything, and everyone, irritates you.

You get frustrated when the convenience store worker insists on double-plastic-bagging your groceries. Plastic everywhere! You fantasize about learning Korean just so you could explain to the woman in line behind you that it doesn't matter how long or short a line is because a line functions in units, not in length, so could she please back up out of your personal space and stop ramming her body into yours? You're so fed up with the world around you that you become nearly homicidal. That was me.

But then, poof! My homicidal homesickness lasted about a month, and it was gone. After four weeks of seriously considering leaving South Korea, I found myself in a *jjimjilbang* (bathhouse) getting a naked scrub-down by a ruthless grandma with loofah gloves and thinking, *Man, my life is cool.* I started going on nightly runs to the local Buddhist temple, where I'd join in on the evening chants (which I couldn't understand, but I'd make humming noises so it still felt somewhat spiritual). I started taking dance classes. Going into the forest more. Going into the city more. When I didn't give in to homesickness, homesickness actually pushed me in the other direction: toward searching for things to fulfill me. Instead of resenting South Korea, I was suddenly loving my life and Korean culture so much that I nearly considered staying for a third year.

Usually, homesickness is temporary. It's valid, but it's still temporary. I had a bad month as a human on planet Earth, and bad days or bad months can happen anywhere. Therefore, when these feelings hit, ask yourself: *Would I rather be having a bad month at home or a bad month here?* That tiny little revelation, that bad months/days/moods will follow you no matter where you go, can help you remain sane in a time of crisis and possibly stop you from making a decision you'd regret later.

Sidenote: South Korea is actually among my favorite places I've ever lived. It's one of the safest destinations in the world for solo female travelers, and I truly cherish the two years I spent there. Don't let my monthlong phase of hating everything deter you from visiting. Definitely go.

Know that I've also gotten sick of Bolivia, Bulgaria, and

Bali. Your mood or mindset is typically *you*-dependent, not country-dependent. I was the problem, not South Korea.

You may reach the point where you're unjustly angry at little things in your day-to-day travel life. You no longer have patience for the cultural quirks or societal oddities you once found humorous — and without humor, happy travel is impossible.

You become stern. You think, *None of this would ever happen back home.*

At home, people mind their manners in public and never speak above a whisper.

At home, no one uses plastic. Only sustainable, eco-friendly, compostable bags.

At home, orderly lines are formed on a red carpet with built-in air-conditioning and lavender mist and a minimum of two feet between all bodies at all times!

At home, the Jonas Brothers clean my house shirtless, and they pay me to allow them the honor.

See? Fetishizing and fantasizing.

SILVER LINING: TRAVEL MAKES YOU APPRECIATE HOME

The longer you're gone, the more you appreciate where you're from. That's a pretty cool silver lining, right? Especially considering the fact that just a few months prior, you were dying to escape your boring-ass, racist-ass, everyone-sucks-here town! But now you realize that there are assholes everywhere and you prefer the assholes in your town. So you decide it's time to go home. Or maybe you still think everyone in your small town sucks and it's finally time to move to the big city when you get home — because if you can hack it in Seoul, you can hack it in San Diego.

Before I left for the Peace Corps, I remember proclaiming, "I just want to go somewhere with culture!" as if America didn't have culture. Now I see that apple pie and the Fourth of July are culture. Manners are also culture, and I no longer subscribe to the rumor that Americans don't have manners. Compared to societies where blowing snot rockets on the floor at a restaurant and physically pushing people out of your way to reach the seafood buffet are considered socially acceptable, I am quite pleased with American manners. Especially when someone says "yes, ma'am" or "bless your heart."

You don't know what you've got 'til it's gone, honey. The things you used to take for granted, you now cherish.

Conclusion: If you hate home, travel. You may discover a new home that suits you better or you may discover your newfound appreciation for your original home — or both!

Fun Fact

The number one thing I now appreciate from home is the ability to drink water out of the tap. It's still such a foreign concept to me that I sip slowly and suspiciously every time I fill my cup with tap water.

WHEN IS HOMESICKNESS A VALID REASON TO ACTUALLY GO HOME?

Getting homesick is normal, yes. But if you're homesick on week number two, fight it. That feeling is just your comfort zone leaving your body. On the other hand, if you are homesick on month number four of a one-way ticket, and you've made a solid effort to either endure it or cure it and you're still miserable, then you might be standing on reasonable grounds to consider going home.

Let me warn you, however: the worst feeling in the world is booking a last-minute flight home only to get home and regret it. Only to get home and miss the place you just left. Only to realize that home was not the solution after all.

✈ **TRAVEL LESSON #18** ···

Don't book emotional flights.

··

Think it through! Don't make quick decisions out of panic or anger. Before you book an escape flight, get a massage or take a nap. Give yourself space between the emotion and the decision. Before you make an unfixable mistake, let me tell you how I fight the urge to flee.

HOW TO BATTLE HOMESICKNESS

◆ **Bust out those homesick letters.** Here's where the homesick letters from chapter 14 will become a godsend! Imagine this: You're having a low-self-esteem day, so you reach for the envelope that says, "You're a Bad Bitch." You're volunteering, but the community doesn't seem to be supporting your initiative to cut down on plastics, so you find the "Keep Going" envelope. On Christmas, you grab the Christmas envelope. On your birthday, you grab many birthday envelopes! You'll be so thankful to have these letters from friends and family from home! They have the power to completely revitalize you during tough times.

- **Know that it will pass.** After my "runner" episode, life moved on in a really beautiful way, as I mentioned. I began studying Korean, and I dabbled in dating an American military guy who had access to Taco Bell on the military base. I found my balance and finished my year in South Korea with love and joy — and tacos!

- **Lean in harder.** Instead of detaching myself from South Korea, I doubled down. In hindsight, I can see that I hadn't been giving 100 percent of my effort to build a happy life for myself, and so my life wasn't 100 percent of what it could have been. I was being lazy and stubborn and wallowing in self-pity rather than actually doing anything about my unhappiness. I was robbing myself of the experience and then complaining about it. Instead of throwing a pity party, get your ass up and rearrange the problem until you find the solution. Or to put it more gently, take a step back and see how you can bedazzle your daily life and weekly routine to awaken the fantasy that brought you here in the first place. Integration is a choice, so choose to dive deeper. Lean into new experiences. Discover what you've been missing. Leave no stone unturned in your hunt for happiness.

- **Call on your emotional-support humans and devil's advocate.** Remember those loved ones you reached out to and elected as your support staff? Now's the time to call them for a lifeline. If you chose these people wisely, your emotional-support humans will give you exactly the pep talk(s) you need to lift you out of your funk; plus, you'll get a rational assessment of your situation from your trusty devil's advocate.

- **Move hotels or islands or cities.** It may not be home

you're missing but comfort and companionship. A change of scenery can quickly fix this. Instead of going home, go to a new location. Move guesthouses or check into a hotel that offers a social element in a location that's walkable! If I can't walk freely to restaurants or shops or through the jungle along the river, I start to feel so alone and isolated. Environment is key.

◆ **Comfort yourself.** Trashy TV, bed, cookies, and Christmas movies. On a down day, allow yourself to give in to the emotions. Cry. Get your nails done. Do something radical like getting bangs or a nose piercing if the mood really calls for it, then move on. Don't let this down day spiral into a down week or a down month — because it can if you let it.

◆ **Practice gratitude.** Remind yourself how lucky you are to be here and how you better adore every moment because this trip won't last forever.

◆ **If all else fails, go home.** If you do decide to cut your trip short and go home, carry no regrets. Life works out how it's supposed to. Trust that whatever choice you make will lead you to incredible things.

When you finally do give in to homesickness and go home, it will be the best feeling in the world.

Fun Fact

I left the Peace Corps six months early, and I'd do it again because it led me to where I am now. But that's a juicy piece of gossip I'll save for a tell-all book or something...

BEFORE YOU FLY HOME

We're not going to pretend that you're going to read this book and never go home again. One day, your one-way ticket will likely be toward the direction you came from. Here are some things I like to do before I return home from a trip.

Give Stuff Away

Before flying home, I give away the things I didn't finish or no longer need, like sunscreen, extra coins, and my book. Once, a girl I traveled with gave me her bathing suit, which I had been admiring, and it became my most cherished travel treasure! Travel mementos are priceless when there is a story behind them.

Another idea: if you happen to pass by a stall selling secondhand clothing, like I often find in Indonesia and Mexico, leave them some good-quality clothes that you think they could resell. This way, you free up space in your bag for souvenirs, reduce your risk of being charged for overweight baggage on the way home, and get to spread some love while traveling more eco-friendly rather than letting your lightly used things go to waste.

Bring Home Some Souvenirs

Take home what the locals eat: candy, snacks, beer, and booze! Head to the local minimart or bodega to bring home some local goodies instead of just the tourist souvenirs like elephant pants from Thailand (although, I love elephant pants as gifts; one size fits all). Check out the beauty products, too. Before you stock up on booze, check how much alcohol you're allowed to bring back before you buy a gallon of mezcal (which may end up getting confiscated)!

Take the New You with You

Every trip is a rebirth. The girl who left is not the same girl who is returning. To make sure you don't slip back into your old ways or lose the beautiful parts of you that you've uncovered, here's a little journaling exercise.

o   What did you discover about yourself on this trip that you admire?

o   How can you bring that into your daily life at home?

o   What don't you want to take for granted ever again?

If you're still not someone who journals, make a point to ponder these questions instead. This is a cathartic exercise to do on the plane or at the airport as you're in that literal transition between home and adventure. As one chapter is closing, a new one begins. When you get home, life will not be the same...

CHAPTER 19

Bummers Back Home

No one warned me. No one told me. No one prepared me for the absolutely paralyzing reality of reverse culture shock, a one-way ticket to a panic attack in public.

REVERSE CULTURE SHOCK

When I flew home from Bulgaria after my first long-term stint living abroad, my sister picked me up at the airport and took me straight to my favorite place on Earth: Target! Not just any Target but a Super Target. I bolted straight to the clothing section. After living in a small post-communist town that still felt slightly communist, I was in heaven!

My sister, sensing that I was content in my natural habitat, told me she was off to do some shopping and for me to come and find her when I was ready. Huge mistake! I hadn't been in America for more than a couple hours at this point. I had gone straight from derelict volunteer life to the airport to Target! Little did I know, I should not have been left unchaperoned...

About three minutes later, my endorphin high started to fade and sensory overload took control. As if the acid had just kicked in, my brain was absorbing all stimuli in HD: every sound, smell, and texture. The aisles around me looked as if they were moving and bending. The chatter of American English pierced into my brain in surround sound. I could understand every single person's conversation, and every conversation bothered me. *Who the hell cares if you have sensitive skin, Debby? Why are you talking about it so loudly as if it's an announcement to the entire store?* But it wasn't just Debby's chatter I was absorbing; it was the chatter of the whole store like voices in my head. I felt schizophrenic. I didn't understand what was happening to me.

This was my first encounter with reverse culture shock.

Here's the thing. In Bulgaria, I spoke Bulgarian and read Bulgarian all day every day. The only time I absorbed English was with my American friends or in the classroom (but let's be real, I spoke Bulgarian there, too). For two years, I had to actively translate conversations and signs. I didn't realize that living abroad offered my brain a filter that allowed me to process or not process the world around me. Like a switch, I could choose to engage or zone out. But suddenly, I was back in my world with my native language, and my brain was processing everything automatically, all at once.

I abandoned my basket and went to find my sister — and then it got worse. Aisle after aisle, I searched for her, but everyone looked the same. I was trying to find a generic white girl in Target in a sea of generic white girls in Target. I distinctly recall stepping into a row of laundry detergent and time slowing down. I was lost in thought. *Why are there twenty brands? Who the fuck needs this many options?* I started to hyperventilate. It was pure America. The people. The consumerism. The unnecessarily loud conversations. A dizzying maze of never-ending things. I felt trapped and I couldn't breathe. I found the bathroom and had my first ever full-blown panic attack. Crying, snot running down my face, short, shallow breaths. And I didn't even have a fucking cellphone to call or text my sister to come find me.

As I left the bathroom, there she was. Checking out, buying $75 more than the bag of chips she came to grab. As soon as she saw me, she knew what was happening.

As we got in the car, I let out sobs of confusion. "I couldn't find you. That store is so big and loud." I was like a five-year-old lost in the mall. "I knew it was too soon to take you there," she said. Call it mother's instinct, my sister knew what I didn't: that after coming from a small town in another land where my options were limited and my neighbors familiar, this experience of overabundance was too much too soon.

In the days following, it wasn't just the consumerism and loud conversations that shook me, but also the nonverbal communication. In Bulgaria, nodding your head up and down quickly, once, means no. And shaking your head left to right means yes (more like *yeah, that's correct*). This is the total opposite in America! My brain would glitch and spasm while trying to nonverbally communicate with people. I'd confuse them and they'd confuse me. Then I'd sit at home, exhausted from acting like a total freak all day long, and legitimately question my ability to reintegrate as an adult in America.

The longer you've been gone and the more foreign the culture you've been immersed in — and especially if you've spent your days speaking a foreign language — the more intense your reverse culture shock may be. My post–Peace Corps experience was pretty extreme, but if you take a trip to Japan for a month to study Japanese, you'll still experience a degree of reverse culture shock. If you work at a school in South Korea for a year, you'll experience a degree of this. If you backpack in Europe or Southeast Asia or South America for a few weeks, you'll experience perhaps a lesser degree but still a degree of this. Coming from Australia, England, or another Western English-speaking country? You'll absolutely notice the differences between environments, and you may find yourself actively comparing cultures, but your brain will most likely be fine. Coming home from a resort in Mexico surrounded by tourists for a week? You won't feel a thing.

Like going from the hot tub to the cold plunge, abruptly switching environments can be a shock. Your body and brain and emotions need time to adjust. The good news is that once you know reverse culture shock is coming, you're less likely to have a meltdown in public. Instead, you let it happen and you let it pass.

✈ **TRAVEL LESSON #19** ·

Prepare for reverse culture shock.

· ·

How? Basically, you need to do everything slowly.

◆ From the airport, go home. Rest for a day.
◆ Let the people you'll be spending the first few days with know ahead of time that you might be sensitive to overstimulation and want to take it easy. Rather than rushing to the Cheesecake Factory or diving into a welcome-home party, you'll need a day to reacclimate.
◆ Shop slowly. Learn from my Target experience. You're going to feel both nostalgia and uneasiness in big, crowded stores.
◆ Then, walk. Walk your neighborhood. Walk your city. Walk a park. I've found walking to be a gentle way to reground myself and remind myself that I'm home.

◆   Finally, accept that you're different from when you left. Home won't feel the same because you're not the same. Every time you travel for an extended period, you discover a new layer of you, which means you access a new layer of life. Embrace the change!

If you've never experienced reverse culture shock, this may sound completely melodramatic. But if you have experienced it, you know exactly what I'm talking about — and hopefully now you feel less crazy.

I will admit, though, I've been living in Seattle for about a year now, off and on, and there are still things that make me feel like an alien or an idiot. My boyfriend's stepmom asked me to set the dinner table, and I had to ask her to show me how. I'd been eating with chopsticks for so long that I forgot which side the knife goes on! Also, when someone asks me a question that requires a quick answer, my brain will glitch, and I'll respond with two words in two languages. And the other day while I was practicing driving, I took a turn and started driving on the wrong side of the road! Safe to say, I'm not yet driving on the freeway. I'm still adjusting.

When you come home, be gentle on yourself. You need time to emotionally and psychologically adjust. Laugh, go slow, and give yourself grace.

That's bummer #1. Now let's discuss bummer #2...

FEELING LIKE A FREAK

Get ready for a welcome-home crew at the airport, reunion dinners, people stopping by to give you an enthusiastic hug, and boys who have always wanted to date you knocking down your door in hopes to take you out. You are the most important person on the planet... until you're not.

You've only got fifteen seconds of fame upon returning home.

Do not be fooled into thinking that this is real life. Your parents may take work off to spend time with you, and your friends might get a babysitter so they can meet you for drinks, but that won't last, darling.

Soon everyone will go back to their busy lives, and you will be faced with the true reality of home. Home is not dinner parties and nights out. Home is a 9-to-5 plus putting kids to bed. Week one might be a party, but by week two, you're old news and your friends have gone back to their busy routines.

Your friends won't want to hear about how you witnessed a coup in Thailand or drank champagne with an ambassador of France. They might think your stories about Prague are pretentious or the fact that you worked for UNICEF is annoying, like you think you're better than them. Your untethered lifestyle feels ostentatious. Your stories become a constant reminder that they wake up to 6 AM alarm clocks and you don't.

They can't relate to your life. Instead, they'll want to talk about their drama, how their neighbor's grass is too long, or how the coffee shop up the street doesn't carry hemp milk so they must be anti-environment and we should cancel that coffee shop!

You may find that you don't enjoy the same people you used to. The Negative Nancies get on your nerves, and the small-minded gossip queens bore you. The surface-level stuff doesn't do it for you anymore. That's because when you travel, your conversations are deep. You meet a total stranger, and instead of talking about the weather, somehow you end up talking about your hopes and dreams and parallel universes and aliens, all within five minutes of meeting each other. You talk about things that matter and mesmerize.

But some people back home aren't ready to think like you. You're the weird one, the flashy one, the woo-woo one. In the presence of people who have never left their bubble, you are too much and not enough all at the same time.

The truth is that you left to find yourself and you did. You changed, but life at home stayed still. You're different, whether they like it or not. For some people, this elevated version of you can be very hard to accept. Some people will want you to dumb yourself down or play small so they can feel big — just wait and see.

Some of your family may judge your inability to sit still and ask what void you're trying to fill by traveling as much as you do, like there's something wrong with wanting to explore new cultures and landscapes. This may leave you feeling misunderstood, like you don't belong. You may begin to feel lost in your own home, likely comparing this life to your travel life and wondering if coming home was the right decision at all.

So how do you adjust? How do you explain to the people at home who are waiting to welcome the old you back that the old you doesn't exist anymore, that the girl who left is not the same girl that's returning? How do you go back home and survive on surface-level conversations? How do you sit around a dinner table and accept that most people would rather talk about themselves than the mysteries and miracles of life? How do you adjust to shallow pools when you've been swimming in the ocean?

Answer: Let some people go.

The Higher Your Vibe, the Smaller Your Tribe

Over time, your circle is going to get smaller. Let it.

I'm not suggesting that you come home from your worldly travels and stop talking to everyone who isn't as worldly as you. If you've got a friend who has never left her hometown and is still working at the Piggly Wiggly but she has a zest for life, is incredibly caring, and can teach you about country thangs like raising ducks and being a good person — hold on to her for dear life! Don't ditch all your friends, but take stock of who you're allowing in your orbit. Reevaluate, and when necessary, cut ties.

Don't forget that you're the girl who has traveled the world. You can make friends anywhere. Don't be afraid of re-stocking your shelf. Cut ties with the people who drag you down, drown you out, and don't let you be yourself. Stop hanging out with the bad influences, the alcoholics, the people who talk about you behind your back, and the toxic energy. Just because you've known someone since kindergarten doesn't mean you're obligated to have a drink with that person every time you come home.

When I used to come home to visit, about half the people I hung around were — gosh, I'm so sorry to say this — going nowhere fast. Drinking their days away, spending money they didn't have, and living for the weekend. They were consumed with victim mentalities, scarcity mindsets, and never-ending excuses to justify staying stuck. Misery loves company, and they were pulling out a seat for me to sit at their miserable table whenever I came home. Eventually, I refused to sit down.

Do You Come from Grayville?

The toughest but best thing I've ever done for myself is dis-tance myself from my family. It's the only family I've ever had, and I've wanted to escape it since I can remember. Watching movies growing up, I always identified with the girls running away from home and finding a new family who loved them and living happily ever after. If you've ever felt the same way, that you needed to escape a toxic family or relationship or social circle, this next bit is for you.

Imagine you are a gray bird that comes from a nest called Grayville. Everyone in your nest is gray, too. Every time you take a trip, however, you return home with a colorful feather. A bright blue one from Nairobi, a golden one from Cape Town — until eventually, you are covered in a colorful rainbow of feathers. The other gray birds will notice. Some will admire your colorful feathers and be inspired! Others will say, "Who does she think she is?" and try to pluck them in hopes of making you gray again.

Some birds are lucky, though, and their flock back home is full of rainbow feathers, too. They don't question the rainbow — they celebrate it!

Where I come from is not like that, though. I come from Grayville. Know that Grayville isn't always a physical place. Sometimes it's a set of expectations or a mindset or a pattern within a place. My Grayville was the house I was raised in. The last time I visited, I took Emilia with me. I went to give my mother one last chance to do better after years of nastiness. Since I was a little girl, I've been trying to save my mother from herself, but as she spiraled deeper and deeper into the dark, she tried to pull me down with her. I escaped, but I held on to hope that I could rescue her, too.

Emilia held my hand as my mother made me feel small. As my mother reminded me that I wasn't special. As she criticized my success, belittled my accomplishments, and laughed at my dreams. And when she berated me in the grocery store, calling me horrible names while I begged her to put the vodka back on the shelf, I knew I couldn't save her, but I could save myself. With the support of my rainbow friend by my side, I made the choice to never return to Grayville. Never return to the painful environment from which I had escaped.

A few days after I cut the cord, my whole life began to fill up with love and success. I met my boyfriend, was adopted into Emilia's family, landed the literary agent of my dreams, was featured in *Forbes*, and got this book deal. Once I stopped living in pain and stopped focusing on how much I hurt — I suddenly had all this positive energy to put toward positive things I've always wanted in my life. Magic.

Your Grayville might be toxic like mine, or your Grayville might be a loving family who created a box to protect you, but the box ended up suffocating you. Your Grayville might be a town of drug addicts or country club members. It might be an absent parent who's never going to show up. We all have a little Grayville to escape. Your feelings about it are all valid. No matter what it looks like from the outside, you know what it feels like on the inside.

As the saying goes, "You are not required to set yourself on fire to keep other people warm."

Once you travel the world, you experience what love feels like. Once you distance yourself from the dark, you can finally see how bright your life is meant to be. Living in Grayville, you're seeing life through a gray cloud. Once you lift up out of that cloud, you see that the world is full of color. And now that you've seen and felt that, you never need to settle for anything less.

Changing your life doesn't happen overnight. It took a decade for me to slowly let go of who was holding me back, but with each trip I took, I gained a clearer perspective on what I was walking away from and why. Just start there. Just start with one trip to give yourself perspective on the relationships you have in your life and see if you can find something that feels safer than that.

Listen to your intuition. You know who needs to go. Don't be afraid of letting them go — be afraid of never escaping them.

We become like the people we surround ourselves with, so surround yourself with people who are smarter, wiser, more interesting, and more ambitious than you (or at least people who give you a run for your money in the above categories). Don't come home to be the smartest girl in the room, the most well-traveled girl in the room, or the most clever girl in the room. The key to leveling up in life is to surround yourself with the people who do it better than you.

Start being selective about the energy you allow into your life. When you come home, bring the girl you created on your trip home with you, and find the people who adore her.

As your circle gets smaller, your relationships with the right people get stronger. The less energy you focus on the negative influences, the more energy is available to focus on the positive influences. It's really that simple, y'all.

Oh, one last bummer for the road! After spending $3 in Thailand on the best green curry you've ever had in your life, you're going to be really pissed to come home and spend $15 on the most mediocre green curry you've ever had in your life. The same goes for Mexican food, Turkish food, and Indian food. You have been warned.

CHAPTER 20

Finding the Best of Both Worlds

I have spent my entire adult life traveling, only returning home long enough to realize that I wanted to leave again. Every time I'd touch down in the States, I'd go through the same familiar cycle: excitement to overwhelm, then underwhelm to leaving again on another one-way ticket to somewhere.

That is, until I met a boy who changed everything. Let me tell you the love story that finally forced me to slow down and stay a while.

Once upon a time, Emilia and I were visiting my hometown. We were writing the new travel guidebook for Seattle, and exploiting men on Bumble to use as tour guides. One night I matched with a guy, and we set up a date. I put minimal effort into my outfit, left the hotel, and met *him*.

After our first date, I was doomed. Totally screwed. I had not intended to fall for a guy who lived in Seattle while I lived all over the world. But whatever, I told myself, it didn't matter because after our third date, I was leaving on a one-way ticket to Mexico, then back to my home in Bali. I could just forget about him and carry on with my life as planned, right? Well, guess who called me every night? And guess who came to see me in Mexico a few weeks later?! And guess who both fell head over heels in love?

When a guy wants to see you, he'll see you no matter where you are. Remember that, ladies.

After chasing one another back and forth from Seattle to Mexico for a few months, I just didn't want to sleep without him anymore. Not because I had fallen for him or because he's super hot, but because when you travel with someone, you feel like you live with them already. You brush your teeth together, you do your laundry together, you go to sleep and wake up together. I wanted to continue to be together. And so I changed my plans and flew to Seattle to be with my boyfriend...who is very private, so I shall refer to him as Mr. Boyfriend from here on out. I unpacked my bag, hung up some clothes, and started playing with the idea of staying a while.

Everyone who has ever known me was in disbelief. The island girl moving to the city? The solo girl accepting a suitor? My friends all doubted my ability to live in the US and "settle down," but I am pleased to announce that I'm totally happy in Seattle!

Except when I'm fucking miserable...

REINTEGRATION CAN BE ROUGH

I have been bouncing between falling in love with my life and feeling like a caged animal since the very beginning of this move. This first year home hasn't been easy. In fact, I'd call it messy.

When you live in a foreign country, each day feels like a video game. There are levels to be unlocked, challenges to conquer, treasures to collect, and codes to crack. The world is an arcade with a never-ending supply of games to play and puzzles to solve. Each time you play a new game, your brain gets hits of dopamine! Your body and nervous system become conditioned to expect that daily surge of feel-good.

Complete a meaningful conversation with your taxi driver in Spanish? Dopamine! Climb down a path to discover the most beautiful waterfall on a Tuesday in Tanzania? Dopamine! Weave your motorbike through Bali traffic on your way to language class? Double dopamine! I received daily doses of dopamine nonstop for over a decade. And then suddenly those daily fixes significantly dropped.

Back home — without surprise, without risk, without unexpected challenges around every corner — I had literal dopamine withdrawals. I unraveled. My body and emotions went into total meltdown for months.

What did I do to replace that dopamine? I'd book a trip, shop way too much, drink every night, eat (or not eat), or do anything that made me feel something! Oh, and I cried a lot. I think, for the first time in my life, I became depressed.

Instead of every day being a thrilling adventure, it became a predictable routine where people live in their predictable bubbles and keep me, the stranger, at a predictable distance.

When you're traveling, all strangers are friends you just haven't met yet. In my boyfriend's bubble, however, I'm the weird homeless girl with a backpack who showed up out of nowhere. I have been here for a year, and while his friends and family have interrogated me plenty, I still feel like I'm taking a test and waiting to pass.

Out in the travel world, you meet a stranger you click with, and the next day you're stuffed together in the back of a minivan surrounded by chickens, talking about your childhood and laughing your ass off.

In Seattle, I feel like I'm walking on eggshells and always

saying the wrong thing. I don't fit in. I don't belong. I have never felt more misunderstood in my life.

Such a harsh change in environment, conversations, and human connection can directly affect your mental health. This move has directly affected my mental health.

It's agonizing to replace nonstop adventure with a sterile routine. I get bored of people's conversations about their cats, I get overwhelmed by grocery stores, I'm still not comfortable driving on the freeway, and I am just having a very difficult time adjusting.

In the past, whenever I felt unfulfilled or overwhelmed, I'd leave. When I knew that there was a cheaper, more exotic, more exciting adventure waiting for me in Thailand or Mexico, it was so easy for me to book a ticket to Bangkok or Puerto Vallarta and begin another wild era of living out of my backpack. And I would. I've always trusted myself. I've always trusted where my intuition would lead me.

But right now, my intuition is doing something crazy.

Here's the catch: When I'm traveling, I miss home; and when I'm home, I miss traveling.

This is a new feeling for me. Maybe it's love, maybe it's my ovaries, maybe it's temporary. No matter what this feeling is, I know I'm not ready to give up on the life I've created with Mr. Boyfriend. I'm not ready to quit this, so I've got to make it work. If I'm going to be home, I've got to figure out how to be happy.

I recently had an almighty *aha* moment that made me stop crying. It sounds so simple, but it was such an epiphany for me. An epiphany that completely changed my perspective on life and travel and the balance between the two.

My big simple epiphany is this: *home is for recharging*.

Home is not supposed to be wild; home is meant to be a

cocoon. This is where I was getting it all wrong. This is where the crying came from. I was trying to make home an unexpected adventure, when home is meant to be stable. For a traveler, home is rest and reflection and Crock-Pots and candles. Home is not meant to be unfamiliar.

If you ever come home and feel out of place after traveling, my advice is this: stop comparing your travel life to your familiar space. Do not put pressure on home to be unexpected. Let home be calm. And hey, even when you're home, don't forget that you live on planet Earth. There are adventures to be had even at home if you choose to see them and seek them.

This one revelation felt like a switch flipped in my brain! I've stopped fighting home and instead have melted into it as my recharging station between trips. So, though I still struggle some days, and I'm not 100 percent sure how this will all play out, I have come up with some tactics that give me the best of both worlds. If you're in a similar place, may these next steps provide a path forward to you, too.

Always Have a Trip on the Calendar

While I'm allowing home to be mellow, I also want to be inspired. The key to my sanity is to always have a trip on the calendar to look forward to. Enjoy home but get ready for what's next. My next epic trip is to Spain, so I'm currently obsessed with all things Spanish (in my head, I say this like *Spain-ish*). I'm practicing the language, creating my bucket list, and mapping out a travel timeline. It's added a sense of pre-adventure into my safe space.

My other pro tip is to realize that travel is not explicitly reserved for trips over the ocean!

For Emilia, living in Spain means that she is just two hours away from a weekend trip to Morocco or France. But over here in North America, we've got an enormous ocean between us and Europe and Asia. I'm not always going to have a month to slip away to the Philippines. It's not practical for me to spend the time and money flying back and forth over the Pacific Ocean five times a year. Yes, there are nonstop flights from Seattle to Central America, but still not quick enough for a reasonable weekend getaway.

So if I want to travel more, I have to travel more creatively. I've gotten into the obvious things: road trips, camping, national parks, small towns, and flying to Mexico whenever I can (even for a week).

House-Sit Close to Home

Here is a hack you might not have thought about when it comes to satisfying wanderlust: house-sitting as staycations. You don't even have to leave your city to travel! Last summer I took a house-sitting gig in a beautiful house just on the other side of Seattle in a neighborhood where I could walk to play pickleball every morning, meet new people, and try new restaurants. I didn't have to completely uproot my life to step into a new reality. By then, I was officially living with my boyfriend in Seattle but craving adventure — so this gave me a mini-dose of solo travel, which allowed me to reconnect with myself and reconnect with my writing. As a creative, I'm always looking for spaces that inspire me, and house-sitting serves as a fabulous inspiration tool. This little getaway even added a fun element to my relationship! My boyfriend would pick me up for date nights, which felt really sexy and fun. Then we'd part and miss each other. By the end of the sit, I was so looking forward to coming back home and had satiated my need for a trip.

Weave Mini-Solos into Your Relationship

If you're a woman with a wild spirit, the person you choose as your significant other is so important — and I chose correctly. I found a person who not only supports my wild spirit but also shares it. Mr. Boyfriend is my second-favorite travel partner, behind Emilia. He is so adventurous and pushes me even further outside my comfort zone when we take trips. We travel the world together, but he also lets me travel alone. Yes, I said, "lets me." As in, he doesn't guilt-trip me for leaving or pressure me to come home. He lets me be me.

Sometimes these mini-solo involve me disappearing on a solo trip while he stays home. Other times, it's us backpacking Vietnam together, then he takes off to trek through a cave while I relax by the river. This gives us a few days to be independent and miss each other.

Weave mini-solos into your relationship and watch how healthy you grow alone and grow together. The way I see it, the more we encourage each other to have a sense of self, the longer we'll last.

However, let's say, I put all this effort into this trial period in Seattle with Mr. Boyfriend and I still don't love it. Then what?

HIT THE ROAD WHEN NECESSARY

I can always leave. A traveler is never stuck. There is always a one-way ticket waiting to take my life to the next level.

I'm not saying to run away when things get hard — but the truth is that I have proved to myself that I can do anything alone. I can eat alone, live alone, be nomadic alone, and dream alone, which means I'm never alone. I can make money from anywhere, and I can always find a place to stay — sometimes a free place to stay — whenever I need. And so I don't rely on anyone but me. It's nice to have a partner in crime or someone to lean on in tough times, but when you learn to lean on yourself, you become unstoppable.

If this whole Seattle thing doesn't work out, my life is not over. I just took a leap of faith and am giving love a chance! I'm not afraid of the future because travel has taught me that there is no such thing as mistakes. In every tough situation, there is always a gift. I know that whatever comes next is meant to be. And all of this is true for you, too.

✈ **TRAVEL LESSON #20** ·······················

Rejection is God's protection.

··

Know that when something doesn't work out for you, it's because something better is waiting. Looking back, it's so clear that every single *no* I received was part of the plan. It's hard to trust the fall now, but in hindsight, you will look back and say, "Oh, I now understand why that didn't work out for me." The breakup, the bummers, the stolen purse — all these letdowns led me to something better. If you don't get that job, if that marriage ends, if you miss that flight — recite, *Rejection is God's protection*, and trust that you are being guided toward something greater.

I hope the advice I've given you above works for you. If you are returning to a place that feels like home, if you have family and friends and roots, my advice *should* work. Let home be calm, let the world be wild. Surround yourself with people who celebrate you, and always have a trip on the calendar.

Maybe you have found, like me, that you're happiest

living out of a backpack, on rickety trains, eating with your hands, toes in the mud, surrounded by people who allow you to be you — happiest when you're exploring the world.

Once you've felt what it feels like to live life *alive*, going through the motions will never be enough for you. My wish for you is that your one-way ticket gives you purpose and perspective that makes your life more meaningful, and that while you may never be able to settle for anything less than a wild adventure again, you will find peace and comfort and new opportunities for growth no matter where in the world you are.

PART FIVE

LIFE IS SHORT

CHAPTER 21

Don't Wait

As I was writing the last chapter, I got a message from a friend in Bali to let me know that my Bali healer, and dear friend, had unexpectedly passed away. Yendri was not a toothless old healer. He was my age and healthy. His death was a total shock. I was supposed to visit him the last time I was in Bali but got busy with errands and thought, *I'll see him next time*. That's the tricky thing about time: we aren't guaranteed more of it. One day will be your last day washing your hair, getting in bed, and falling asleep. Not maybe. Certainly.

One day you, too, are going to die. As in, one day you will no longer be on this Earth. You will no longer have the chance to drink beer at Oktoberfest, celebrate Día de los Muertos in Oaxaca, or study Mandarin in Taiwan because you won't be alive anymore. Maybe your spirit will go to heaven, maybe you'll come back reincarnated as a miniature pony, maybe this is all just a simulation, but one thing is for sure: you will never live this life in this body at this moment in time ever again.

And if that's not enough to scare you, here are a few things that should:

- ◆ Venice, Italy, is sinking.
- ◆ The Maldives are slowly being submerged.
- ◆ The Great Barrier Reef off Australia is disappearing.

Go before you or everything on your bucket list is gone.

So now let's pretend that you have just five years left to live. What are you going to do in the next five years? Are you going to die with stories about waterfalls, fireflies, spiritual experiences, and crocodiles? Or are you going to die with stories about doing laundry and stress-eating on the couch in the company of five cats?

Don't waste another day! Apply for that job, dump that deadbeat boyfriend, and book that flight!

✈ **TRAVEL LESSON #21** ·····································

Don't be afraid of letting go — be afraid of never going.

··

This book is dedicated to Yendri.

CHAPTER 22

We Need a Revolution

What if we flipped the script on what young women are supposed to do after high school and college? Instead of expecting them to get married, have babies, or be pushed into a career that looks good on paper, what if we sent our girls on a mission to discover who they are first? What if we normalized travel as a prerequisite for making the biggest decisions (and/or mistakes) of their lives?

Haven't backpacked Southeast Asia yet? You're not ready to get married!

Haven't surfed in Sayulita yet? Don't go to law school until you do!

What if we stopped looking at travel as self-indulgent playtime and saw travel as a necessary path toward living a fulfilled life? Would we be less likely to enter marriages destined for divorce and jobs that end in mental breakdowns? I sure think so.

Once on that path, what if we took it a step further and normalized travel as therapy? Because that's what travel is. Travel is therapy. Travel is medicine. Travel is rebirth.

In your twenties and going through a breakup? Go heal your heart in Bali.

In your thirties and feeling burned-out at work? You need a break before you break! Sail around Greece.

In your forties and getting divorced? It's time to rediscover who you are and what you want to do next. Backpack Europe.

In your fifties and tired of being a good girl? Go find a lover in Puerto Rico and dance the nights away.

And if you're happy as a clam in a relationship that brings you joy, remember that you still have to learn to love yourself, heal yourself, and know yourself. No relationship can do that for you.

I know I talk about love a lot, but travel has never been about finding a partner to complete you. You complete you. Which is going to make you a great partner, ironically. One day you will find love. You are a catch, after all! Just make sure that whoever you choose encourages you to stay wild and free.

ONE MORE THING TO NORMALIZE: TRAVELING MOMS

I cannot tell you how many European couples I see backpacking Southeast Asia with their babies. Climbing on boats, trains, and planes with a kid strapped to their front and two more trailing behind. The Europeans understand that you don't have to bubble-wrap your children! Repeat after me: *Travel will not break your kids!* Just the opposite. Travel will help you raise brilliant, empathetic, curious human beings who grow up to be incredible adults!

I've also met plenty of moms who are on solo trips. Shout-out to all the moms who are showing their kids that self-love and personal development never have to end. These moms are role models of how to never lose your sense of self no matter what stage of life you're in. Your kids aren't watching you leave — your kids are seeing you go! You are setting a dazzling example, and your children will likely follow in your footsteps as they grow. Stay curious, moms. I'm sure that if my mother treated herself better, she would have treated me better. Love yourself, and that love will trickle down.

And hey, if you plan to never get married or never have kids — I support you! Women don't live in a box anymore. Do whatever you want.

ONE-WAY FOREVER

My money will forever be spent on travel and experiences, not things. This is how the "new rich" spend their money. Instead of owning the hottest car, we want to go wine tasting in France. Instead of the Gucci bag, we want plane tickets. Instead of showing off, we want spiritual healing.

You may weave some normalcy into your life, but no matter whether you move to Spain with your soul mate or decide to return home and raise a family with your high school sweetheart, you will never truly "settle down." Once you've tasted the thrill of a one-way ticket, there is no other way to satisfy that craving for adventure, and that's okay. With remote work becoming ever more common; with women making more money, having fewer children, and having them later in life; with your newfound passion; with this book — you can customize your life how you dream it to be! Screw settling down. Screw clocking in Monday through Friday. To hell with waiting until you're retired to travel the world or pursue a passion. Live life now!

✈ **TRAVEL LESSON #22** ·····························

The best adventures start with the simple decision to go.

You can do this, and you can do this alone! If you follow this book with faith and action, you will be sitting outside in new air eating a new food watching a new sunset sooner than you think.

Do not let this book sit on your desk or live in your phone while you wait for it to magically burst into plane tickets. That's never going to happen. You've got to take the first step. Decide right now that you're going to go…somewhere.

STILL HAVE NO IDEA WHERE YOU'RE GOING TO GO FIRST?

Then let's start with one clear, intentional, transformative mission…

Your mission is to fly to the other side of the world and learn to eat alone.

I believe that every woman should travel solo if only to learn how to eat alone and love it. To get dressed up and date herself in a foreign city with a foreign menu, stumbling over a foreign language.

The first dinner is awkward, of course. You feel self-conscious being the lonely lady in a room full of couples and groups. But soon, you begin to look forward to eating alone. To sip your wine as the mysterious woman in the corner of a candlelit restaurant, content in her own company. You take a chance on the menu and order things you've never even heard of, just to surprise yourself. You even order dessert. You treat yourself how you've always wanted to be treated. You finally embrace that, alone, you can go wherever and be who-ever you want.

Soon, you no longer endure being alone. You look forward to it, to the delight of sitting by yourself in a place where no one knows you, thinking, *I did this for me.*

So that is where I'd start, with dinner. Read this book, pick a restaurant in a country on your bucket list, and go to dinner on the other side of the world alone.

When you're ready to really start planning that first dinner, meet me on my website at Alexa-West.com/OneWay, where you'll find a library of resources covering everything we've discussed in this book. You'll also find meditations, pep talks, and soothing rituals for when you're freaking out. So stick with me and let's grow into the future together. You and me, we're not over yet.

Your Final Homework

Please write me and let me know what incredible adventure you decide to chase. Tell me where you're going and what you're doing. I want to hear your story. Send me a travel love letter at Alexa@Alexa-West.com and tag me in your Instagram posts and stories @SoloGirlsTravelGuide.

Your Other Final Homework

Pass it on. If this book has inspired you, contribute to the movement of encouraging women to go find themselves and have their travel experiences. Get another copy of *The One-Way Ticket Plan* and give it to your sister, your mom, or your lunch lady. Have her read it. Now you have someone to share your dreams with.

This book has landed in your life for a reason. You're supposed to go. So go. Trust yourself, follow your heart, and just book that ticket already (one-way, preferably).

The 11 Travel Commandments

1. **Be an explorer, not a tourist.** Some people travel just for the photos, while others travel to find the unfamiliar, connect with strangers, expand their minds, and try new things for the sake of trying new things. Which kind of traveler are you?

2. **Leave room for happenstance.** Don't overstuff your itinerary. Slow down, be where you are, and leave space for serendipity.

3. **Vote with your dollar.** When possible, choose to support local businesses that operate ethically: those that respect the environment, benefit their local communities, don't take advantage of animals or humans, and treat their staff really well.

4. **Look for the gift.** Love your mistakes! With every bump in the road comes a gift. Miss a bus? Look for the gift. Lose your room key? Look for the gift. Get dumped on your honeymoon? Look for the gift! There will always be a gift if you're willing to see it.

5. **Stay curious.** Ask questions! Ask them when you like something and ask them when you don't understand something. Out loud or in your head. And whenever you feel judgment arising in you, replace it with a question instead.

6. **Learn a little language.** If you can speak ten basic phrases in the local language, you will avoid the

tourist traps, get better prices, find better food, make friends with the coconut man on the corner, and unlock layers of life that most tourists cannot.

7. **Count experiences, not passport stamps.** You can never "do" Mexico. You can go to Mexico fifty times, and each experience will be different than the last. Travel to live, not to brag.

8. **Mind your impact.** Leave every place better than you found it. Take a piece of trash from the beach and be kind to people you meet. Bring your own water bottle, canvas bag, and reusable straw to avoid single-use plastics.

9. **Avoid unethical voluntourism.** People are not zoo animals. Playing with children at orphanages, temporarily teaching English in villages, or volunteering at women's shelters can hurt more than they help.

10. **Carry your positivity.** Ever have a lousy day, then a stranger smiles at you and flips your entire mood? Travel can be hard, but positivity is your secret weapon. Happy vibes are contagious. Even when you don't speak the local language, a smile or a random act of kindness tips the universal scale in the right direction for you and the people you meet along your journey.

11. **Trust your gut.** Listen to that little voice inside you. When something doesn't feel right, back away. When something feels good, lean in. Your intuition will lead you to beautiful places, unforgettable moments, and new lifelong friends.

Acknowledgments

One day, my healer Gaby said to me, "Lexi, you need to go home and tape a bunch of big pieces of paper around your room. There is a book waiting to be born." Like a crazy person, I covered my room in paper. Over the next few months, I'd spring out of bed in the middle of the night or drop my burrito and sprint to my bedroom when an idea came to me. I'd write it all on the walls until finally this book made sense. Gaby, thank you for teaching me how to connect to the Universe and listen to myself.

To my best friend and travel sister, Emilia: Let's be real. I wouldn't be where I am today without your unconditional friendship, pep talks, and daydream sessions. Life is absolute magic with you in it. Creativity, laughter, and *chisme*, forever and ever.

To my dream agent, Michele Martin: Thank you for believing in me. Thank you for your never-ending wisdom and guidance. To my editors at New World Library, Georgia Hughes and Kristen Cashman: It's like you took this book and sprinkled magical powers on it. I'm in awe.

To my friends who read, edited, contributed, and told me the truth, Sharon, Meagan, Melissa, Joi, Jen, Judy, Kaitlin, MJ, and Sunny: Thank you for being the godmothers of this book.

To my writing sanctuaries, Four Seasons Resort Punta Mita, Four Seasons Resort Los Cabos at Costa Palmas, W Seattle, The

Maxwell Hotel, and Shinta Mani Angkor: Thank you for holding space for me to dream and write (and eat).

To every single traveler who has ever sent me a message of love and support: Thank you. Your messages mean the world to me. I love hearing your stories and being a part of your journey. You are why I do what I do.

Finally, to pickleball: I love you more than life itself.

Index

About the Author

Alexa West is a bestselling travel author and hotel reviewer who teaches women how to travel the world without going broke or getting kidnapped. In 2011, Alexa left Seattle on a one-way ticket with just $200 in her pocket — and turned that into over ten years of full-time travel. She went from budget backpacker to solo female travel expert — and now teaches thousands of women how to travel alone and make money from anywhere. Best known as the founder and creator of The Solo Girl's Travel Guide, the number one travel guidebook series for women, Alexa is changing the way women travel the world: with less fear and more fun. Through her travel books, blog, online communities, clubs, courses, and female-only trips, Alexa has garnered thousands of fans across the globe. She has been featured by *Forbes* and *USA Today*, and her books have appeared in productions including HBO's *Curb Your Enthusiasm*. Alexa currently splits her time between Seattle, Mexico, and Southeast Asia, where she continues to pursue her love of travel, hotels, pickleball, and writing.